Police
Cars

Malcolm Bobbitt

SUTTON PUBLISHING

Sutton Publishing Limited
Phoenix Mill · Thrupp · Stroud
Gloucestershire · GL5 2BU

First published 2001

Cover photographs: *Front*: S-type Jaguars
were used by a number of police forces,
including the Met. (*Metropolitan Police
Museum*) *Back*: Rover V8 3500 patrolling
the motorways of the West Midlands in the
1970s. (*Colin Chipperfield Collection*)

British Library Cataloguing in Publication Data
A catalogue record for this book is available from the
British Library.

ISBN 0-7509-2510-8

Typeset in 10.5/13.5 Photina.
Typesetting and origination by
Sutton Publishing Limited.
Printed and bound in England by
J.H. Haynes & Co. Ltd, Sparkford.

To many people the Jaguar is the archetypal police car, and to others it might be a Wolseley or
Rover. Pictured in 1966 soon after it entered service with Manchester City Police, this MkII
saloon is crewed by two women officers, the driver having passed the necessary advanced driving
test to enable her to take charge of the vehicle. At a time when in some areas of the country it
was unusual to employ women police drivers, in Manchester this was accepted practice. Jaguars
featured in many constabularies and were used on Traffic patrols as well as for motorway duties.
It was customary for some police forces to specify cars with lesser levels of trim than would
otherwise be seen on a Jaguar, and for the rear seats to be removed to accommodate the large
amount of kit, including cones and signs which, by necessity, were carried. Some vehicles had
modified engines which afforded even better performance than production models. (*Greater
Manchester Police Museum*)

Contents

Acknowledgements

This book would not have been possible without the help of the following people who have contributed information and photographs. In particular I would like to thank Bob Cox, Paul Dew and Ray Seal (Metropolitan Police Museum); Mike Head and Sergeant Andy Stephenson (Driver Training, Cumbria Constabulary); Duncan Broady (Greater Manchester Police Museum); Roger Blaxall (Lancashire Constabulary); Kelvin Brown and Fran Chamberlain (Ford Motor Company); Debbie Shields and Dennis Shearer (Vauxhall Motors); Marie Tieche, Mike Budd and Jonathan Day (National Motor Museum); Colin Chipperfield, Richard Mann, John Pickersgill, Stan Turbitt and Martin Bourne. In addition my thanks to the many constabulary officers and retired police personnel who have willingly provided so much in the way of material. Finally, my thanks are extended to Rupert Harding at Sutton Publishing for his encouragement and forbearance, and to my wife Jean for her usual tolerance and enthusiasm during months of research and foraging among archive material.

Malcolm Bobbitt, Cumbria, 2001

The Met entered this Wolseley 6-99 in the 1960 Monte Carlo rally. The crew, driver E.C. Gahan (at the wheel) and co-driver H.J. Shillabeer (by the nearside door) were both based at Hendon Driving School. The officer in the foreground is a member of the support team and unfortunately he is not identified. How the team and crew fared in the event alas was not recorded. H.J. Shillabeer participated in the Monte in 1956 when the Met entered a Humber Super Snipe. (*Metropolitan Police Museum*)

Foreword

COLIN CHIPPERFIELD

Associate of the Greater Manchester Police Museum, Police Vehicle Enthusiasts' Club Specialist and member of the Police History Society

At last! This illustrated publication, which traces the history and development of police transport over the last one hundred years or so, is one that I and many others have for long been waiting.

Malcolm Bobbitt has provided the essential information largely concerning police cars from the early 1900s, touching on the black and largely inconspicuous cars of the inter-war and immediate post-war years with their 'police' plate and bells, to today's highly visible and audible state-of-the-art vehicles.

It is interesting to note that in attempting to provide police transportation at as low a cost as possible (a situation that prevails to this day), pedal and motorcycles, along with three-wheelers, were once the norm. The increasing use of cars by criminals dictated change, hence the creation of the Flying Squad in 1918. As reliance upon motor cars became widespread, so it was necessary to introduce traffic policing and for the police to keep abreast of vehicle developments.

It is not only the cars that changed over the years: there have been enormous developments in the special equipment which police vehicles carry. When warning bells were introduced, their use was greeted with reluctance by some constabularies who argued that the standard traffic horn, as fitted by the vehicle manufacturer, was adequate for their needs. Despite changing attitudes, the siren, as used in America, was once considered too loud for the British public. The modern police car bristles with innovative technology, to the extent it serves as a mobile incident unit.

With the advent of roadside speed detection equipment, together with the recent revolutions in communications systems technology, the question of the future role of police vehicles is often raised. The progressive use of cameras and satellite tracking devices suggests that there will be a substantial reduction in the number of traffic cars, thus transferring police personnel to beat duties, although the requirement for rapid response vehicles will remain.

Modern policing makes increasing use of helicopters and fixed-wing aircraft, both of which have proved to be invaluable in the tracking and pursuit of target vehicles, particularly on motorways, as well as affording greater safety to the general public.

What future technological miracles are in store is anyone's guess. With the possibility of traffic grinding to a complete halt, gridlock in major towns and cities, we may yet see the return of the bobby on the bicycle!

Bedford police coaches were a familiar sight in London and the Home Counties during the early post-war years. This example is seen leaving the Met's Training School at Hendon in 1949. (*Vauxhall*)

Introduction

I am of an age to remember when, as a child in London, police cars seemed, almost without exception, to be Wolseleys. Their demanding role gave the marque, with its illuminated oval badge, a distinct reverence and when those panther-like machines sped along the streets of the capital, the shrill bells piercing the noise of traffic, it was an occasion. Post-war austerity meant that car ownership was less widespread than it was a couple of decades later and traffic congestion was nowhere near what it is today.

A squad car in full flight evoked a measure of romanticism: the 'Men In Blue' in pursuit of bandits or on a mission of mercy was nothing less than heroic. Sometimes there would be two cars, occasionally three, and that would be the talking point of the day. Police stories were popular then, as they still are; films and television portrayed virtual propaganda with *Dixon of Dock Green*, *Fabian of the Yard* and Inspector Lockhart of *No Hiding Place*. Then came *Z Cars* with its gritty portrayal of policing in an imaginary new town on Merseyside.

Police cars were invariably black, or so it seemed. The Home Office thought they should stay black, but some constabularies, led by Lancashire, considered otherwise. Black changed to white, sirens replaced bells and blue flashing lamps, together with reflective side stripes, made vehicles all the more conspicuous, by day and night. Britain's motorway network grew at the same time as new urban areas sprang up and there was pressure on the police to place more and more reliance upon motor vehicles.

The police car as we know it is a relatively recent aspect of policing. Certainly, the arm of the law had interest in motor vehicles from their inception and there is evidence that cars were commandeered by police in events of emergency. Cars were sometimes used by senior officers, but the role of the motor vehicle was not universally appreciated by the police service.

The First World War was responsible for a change in attitudes. After the war, the Flying Squad, equipped initially with a motley fleet of wartime lorries, was formed to curb a rapidly escalating crime rate. It was another decade before police patrol cars, amid much suspicion, became a familiar sight on British roads. The introduction of traffic patrols was recognition of Britain's increasing dependence upon motor transport and the resulting traffic congestion, alarming accident figures and often poor standards of driving, all of which had given successive governments cause for concern.

Social conditions as well as technological advances have also determined the evolution of police cars. Whereas wireless was once considered a scientific break-through in communications, today's vehicles have highly sophisticated equipment, including satellite tracking. Modern police cars often clock up extraordinary mileages and they are expected to be reliable and responsive to situations. However, we must not forget those highly skilled officers who spend their working lives at the wheel.

In telling the story of British police cars it has been necessary to include some policing history, if only to illustrate the reasons for change and development. In so doing, the following pages contain much about some well-loved motor cars, including Wolseleys with their distinctive radiators, Rileys, with their blue diamonds and MGs with their famous octagonal mascots. Rovers, especially the 3500 and its successor the SDI find a place as well as Vauxhalls and Humbers. Such a book would be incomplete without those highly respected S-type and XJ6 Jaguars; Ford Zephyrs of the 1960s, Land Rovers, Range Rovers and the Panda car which was once an essential part of Unit Beat Policing. Neither have I forgotten the many support vehicles, among them the Black Marias.

When it was first suggested I write this book, the project appealed to me immensely. Following some extensive research which involved meeting and talking to a considerable number of serving and retired police service personnel, as well as police vehicle enthusiasts, that interest, I am happy to write, did not diminish. On the contrary, I quickly realized what an enormous task I had taken on, and thus I found myself immersed in a wholly compelling subject, much of which has remained unrecorded and overlooked.

In compiling this volume I have endeavoured not to be too technical, nor have I succumbed to the temptation to dwell on the vagaries of intricacy. It is often the subject of debate within specialist groups whether particular vehicles of specific constabularies employed slightly varying light boxes or decals. The aim, therefore, has been to enkindle nostalgia. My opening words, in presuming all police cars to be Wolseleys and often black at that, could not have been further from the truth!

Malcolm Bobbitt
Cumbria, 2001

1

Black Marias and Horseless Carriages

When policing as we know it today was introduced in Britain, the motor vehicle had yet to be invented. Sir Robert Peel's brigade of uniformed police first took to the streets in 1829, some seventy years after the volunteer force of Bow Street Runners had been established to catch thieves and reduce rising crime. The most usual means of getting about was either on foot or by horse, stage coaches, horse-drawn omnibuses and cabs were slow and uncomfortable. Generally, roads were unmade; those in rural areas were mostly pot-holed, dusty when dry and puddled when wet, while in towns and cities they were often narrow and congested. While the role of the police was to prevent crime, ultimately duties became all the more diverse. Not all parts of the country were provided with such an effective policing system as London. It was not until the mid-1850s, when the County & Borough Police Act was implemented, that the whole of Britain benefited from government sponsored police forces.

The history of policing in Britain goes back further than the force Sir Robert Peel established when he was Home Secretary in Lord Liverpool's government from 1822. Although 'policing' *is* used in the loosest of terms, 'constables' were a feature of British life as early as the thirteenth century. They were responsible for the good behaviour of a parish or commune and made regular reports to local courts concerning offenders. The Statute of Winchester, in 1285, made provision for boroughs to appoint Watches, usually comprising a dozen men; smaller towns had Watches of between four and six men, depending upon the population. Constables often performed other roles in society as well as policing; they may have been churchwardens and sometimes their duties included supervising an area's poorest inhabitants or surveying highways. Early policing was two-tiered, the constables, or watchmen, reported to justices of the peace, usually members of the county gentry, who were appointed by the crown. Nevertheless, policing was low profile and therefore posed little deterrent to crime and disorder, which was generally rife.

Nowhere in Britain was the crime rate so great as in London. This is hardly surprising, considering the capital was the most densely populated part of the British

Isles, having some 670,000 inhabitants in 1700, the figure rising to over a million within a century. To put these figures into a proper perspective, one in ten people in England lived in the metropolis. We can thank Sir Thomas De Veil and Henry and Sir John Fielding, for alerting society to the dreadful state of crime in the capital. During the late 1730s De Veil established a centre for the administration of justice in the City of Westminster, at Bow Street magistrates' office. His ideas for containing crime and disorder were ambitious and following his death in 1746, the novelist Henry Fielding (1707–54) was appointed principal justice for the City of Westminster in his place. The post was then occupied by Sir John Fielding on Henry's death.

The Fielding brothers were responsible for employing a group of professional thief-takers who assisted in the detection and capture of offenders, the group becoming known as the Bow Street Runners. The patrol, which by 1791 was uniformed, gradually grew in size until two units of a dozen officers undertook twelve hour round-the-clock watches. By the end of the century most parishes in London operated similar schemes and as many as seventy men, all based at Bow Street, supervised the main routes into the City of London from evening until midnight. The numbers of Bow Street Runners increased over the decades so that by 1830 almost 300 officers and men patrolled London's streets. Significantly, horses were introduced to assist in the battle against crime.

As well as the Bow Street Runners, a number of private police forces were set up. One such was instigated by a group of West India merchant men, the aim of which was to protect goods on ships while on the River Thames. It was this police group, absorbed by the government in 1800, which emerged as the Thames River Police.

When he became Home Secretary in 1822, Peel urged Parliament to agree the formation of a proper police force. This did not happen immediately, nevertheless, Peel managed to guide legislation successfully through Parliament. In 1829 constables of the Metropolitan Police began patrolling beats in the capital. Compared with the system that the Metropolitan Police replaced, it was ten times larger and comprised some 3,000 constables. Peel had deliberately set out to devise a force that had strict discipline, including compulsory uniforms, though the style was designed to be quite dissimilar to that of the military. Unlike infantrymen, members of the Metropolitan Police force were issued with uniforms consisting of a top hat and a blue swallow-tail coat. Neither was weaponry as sophisticated as that provided for soldiers: constables carried wooden truncheons, although in extreme circumstances cutlasses were issued for riot control or when patrolling a beat known to be particularly dangerous. Firearms, usually pocket pistols, were only issued to inspectors and senior officers.

Peel appointed two police commissioners, Richard Mayne and Colonel Charles Rowan, both of whom operated from an office in Scotland Yard. However, it took a full decade before policing was seen to be to effective. During this period it was proposed to amalgamate both the horse patrol and the river police with the Metropolitan Police to form a single authority.

The success of the Metropolitan Police was noted outside London and reforms for policing the provinces became an urgent issue. Already some local authorities were calling upon the Metropolitan Police for assistance, especially to quell the Anti-Poor Law disturbances of the 1830s. On some occasions members of the Metropolitan

Police were requested to form an infrastructure for the establishment of local authority policing.

Peel made it known that he favoured provincial policing to be on similar lines to those in London, something which often evoked violent hostility. A number of towns and cities, including Manchester, resented any idea that policing might be governed or influenced by London. Nevertheless, the need for effective provincial policing was uppermost in the concerns of all local authorities. In 1832 the then Home Secretary, Lord Melbourne, prepared a bill for the provision of a police system throughout the country. Despite the bill being abandoned, the will for reform remained. Four years later, when Melbourne was Prime Minister, the Home Secretary, Lord John Russell was persuaded by the reformist Edwin Chadwick to appoint a Royal Commission to report on proposals for a rural constabulary.

The Rural Constabulary Act of 1839, together with amendments to the act a year later, placed the responsibility for rural policing on county magistrates. There were exceptions however. Responsibility for policing in Birmingham, Bolton and Manchester was directed to each of the cities' local authorities. The authorities in Birmingham were not keen on the idea, a situation which ultimately led to rioting and calling on the Metropolitan Police to help quell the disturbances.

The role of the Metropolitan Police and the structure of its organization did have a substantial influence on establishing provincial forces. The Municipal Corporations Act of 1835, whereby town councils were obliged to provide uniform procedures for the electorate, was most influential in determining policing needs and by the end of the 1830s most towns and boroughs had complied with statute requirements.

During Victorian times policing emerged as very diverse. As well as controlling disturbances and preventing crime, the police searched for missing persons, installed soup kitchens and supplied clothing for the poorest in the community; responsibility also fell to the police to arrange summer excursions for the most needy children. The police were trained to administer first aid to members of the public involved in accidents or who were victims of violence and by 1884 most police stations in London were equipped with stretchers and ambulances. Police surgeons were appointed and those police stations nearest to rivers were supplied with life-saving facilities including fire-fighting. Some duties were considered a burden to effective policing, such as collecting market tolls, the inspection of weights and measures and river watching, under the Salmon Fishery Act, to prevent poaching. As road traffic increased more police were employed on traffic regulation. In Birmingham, for example, police officers were responsible for the inspection of tramcars, while in London the Metropolitan Police assumed supervision of the Public Carriage Office. Before motor cars and taxi cabs, police officers were obliged to have an understanding of hackney carriages which, being horse-drawn, meant a knowledge not only of cab construction, but the ailments usually associated with horses.

However, it was not only in the capital that increasing numbers of vehicles had become a concern during the nineteenth century. Throughout Britain all main city roads were clogged with horse-drawn vehicles and scenes similar to those depicted by the artist Gustave Doré were witnessed, although it has to be said that some artistic licence existed. In London, traffic congestion was lessened with the coming of railways and the Underground.

Until 1900 policing was very much a pedestrian activity, although horse patrols were employed in London and other large towns. Some horse-drawn cabs were reserved for conveying chief constables and senior officers, while other more workaday types of carriage, usually four-wheel 'growlers' similar to those in use in London as hackney carriages, were used to transport constables to their duty positions. Black Marias, the familiar nickname given to horse-drawn prison vans, were a regular sight and it was customary to see them being used to round up vagabonds and criminals before they were carted off to jail or police cells. In name the Black Maria has survived to the present day, though modern vehicles are either painted white or in a constabulary's corporate colours. Exactly how the Black Maria received its appellation is unclear, although reliable sources suggest that prison vans took the name of a female offender who was frequently picked up by the police.

Overall responsibility for maintenance of the law fell to the Home Office, which, since the Victorian period, has been increasingly involved in regulating social conditions. While the Metropolitan Police fell directly within the Home Secretary's control, elsewhere policing was the responsibility of borough and county authorities, with only minimal Home Office supervision. Only in extreme situations, such as magistrates requesting military assistance, would the Home Secretary be involved in such drastic measures as authorizing the dispatch of troops.

The arrival of the motor car late in the nineteenth century had a crucial impact upon society. Unlike steam engines, the internal combustion engine was easily manageable and in contrast to steam vehicles, the petrol-driven car was far more manoeuvrable and sociable. Its introduction had been thwarted, to a great extent, by laws, which meant that other European countries were able to experience the joys of motoring well before the cacophony of the internal combustion engine was heard in Britain. This is why motoring in Britain was initially influenced by the Germans and French and why the few motor cars that plied our roads were mainly Daimlers, Benz, De Dion-Boutons, Panhard et Levassors, Peugeots and Renaults. Pioneering motorists on mainland Europe were largely free of the restrictions imposed in Britain where car owners were made to comply with the Light Locomotives on Highways Act of 1865. All machine-powered vehicles were limited to a speed of 4mph and 2mph while travelling through villages and towns. Moreover, each vehicle had to be accompanied by three persons, one walking twenty yards ahead carrying a red flag warning of impending danger. Before 1896 the few cars that were in use were subject to those laws governing steam traction engines.

As it was a criminal offence to exceed the speed limit, the police became the adversary of the motorist from an early date. Those pioneering automobilists who exceeded the speed limit were known as 'scorchers'. Among the most notable scorchers was Walter C. Bersey, a designer of electric vehicles who introduced the first motorized taxi cabs to London, known as 'hummingbirds' because of the motor's high-pitched sound. Bersey was summoned to appear in court in 1896 only a few days before the repeal of the act. Needless to say, pioneering motorists were mostly a gregarious lot for whom speed was a thrilling adventure. James Gordon Bennett, publisher of the *New York Herald*, donated a silver trophy to encourage international motor sport. Other prominent people who strove to establish ever greater speeds include The Hon C.S. Rolls, Selwyn Edge, Charles Jarrot, Léon Serpollet, the Hon Evelyn Ellis and Camille Jenatzy.

The Red Flag Act, until its repeal, held back any real prospect of a flourishing British motor industry. When the speed limit rose from 4mph to 14mph on 14 November 1896 (local authorities reduced this to 12mph where it was considered appropriate) the entrepreneur Harry J. Lawson organized a celebratory run for motor cars from London to Brighton to commemorate the occasion, the event being enthusiastically maintained today. For most car owners though, even 14mph was restrictive and consequently vigorous campaigning in Parliament ensued. On 1 January 1904 the Motor Car Act 1903 came into force. The intention was to abolish speed restrictions on open roads, but ultimately an overall speed limit of 20mph was imposed and remained in force until the end of 1930. It also became a legal requirement for all motorists to obtain a driving licence and for all motor vehicles to carry a number plate; dangerous driving became an indictable offence. Third party insurance and eye sight tests for drivers became regulatory from 1 January 1931, as did driving tests for disabled motorists. Compulsory driving tests for all motorists were introduced in May 1931.

At first, car ownership in Britain was almost exclusively the domain of the aristocracy and the wealthy. As well as those already mentioned, names which became synonymous with motoring included Lord Northcliffe, the Hon. John Edward Douglas-Scott-Montagu MP (the future 2nd Baron Montagu of Beaulieu), Fred Lanchester, Thomas Humber, William Riley, Frederick Simms and Claude Johnson. Often bicycle manufacturers diversified from two wheels to four. The hub of Britain's motor industry developed around Coventry and the Midlands, home of the cycle industry. However, despite its convenience, comfort and speed, the automobile was viewed by many as an unwelcome intrusion. There is little evidence that constabularies in Britain saw the motor car as a means of improving policing methods and for some time, its advantages remained largely ignored.

Accidents involving motor vehicles were commonplace. John Vassilli was possibly the first pedestrian to be killed when he was struck by a car, owned by the Bradford Motor Company, on 15 April 1898 in Scarborough. The first recorded fatal accident was in February 1899 at Harrow-on-the-Hill when a Daimler, which was being tested by the Army & Navy Stores, suffered a collapsed axle when braking heavily on Grove Hill. The driver, Edwin Sewell, along with one of the five passengers, Major Ritchie, died. The accident was witnessed by J.T.C. Moore-Brabazon, later Lord Brabazon of Tara, who was then a young pupil at Harrow School; later he went on to have a career in motoring and aviation.

The battle lines between police, who were responsible for maintaining the law and motorists, who were determined to travel at ever increasing speeds, was quickly defined. The so-called 'Emancipation Act' of 1896 had clearly stipulated a speed limit and motorists felt aggrieved at being prosecuted for exceeding it, especially when stop-watches used to enforce the law were considered unreliable. The Automobile Association was formed in 1905 expressly to warn motorists of speed traps, a practice which was outlawed within a year. However, devious means of informing drivers of speed traps remained. Members were instructed by the AA to stop patrolmen who did not salute, whereupon they were advised to 'drive slowly in accordance with road conditions'. However, speed trap patrols existed before the AA. As early as 1901 the importers of Panhard et Levassor cars were operating an additional service to one conducted by the Brighton Road Motor Patrol to warn motorists of police presence. The BRMP used motor cars and cycles fitted with red flags to alert drivers of speed traps on what was one of the most frequently used roads in Britain. In addition, both *The Autocar* and *The Motor* published details of various traps.

The advent of the motor car meant that police, who remained faithful to foot and horse power, were at a disadvantage. Constabularies were painfully slow to adopt motor cars, and in some instances even bicycles were discouraged. In some police forces there was universal disregard and aversion to motor cars, despite their widening appeal and use. There is no denying that the police were very often hostile towards owners of motor vehicles and knowing that magistrates and large numbers of the general public shared a distrust of drivers and their machines, they were alert to securing convictions against motorists whenever possible. There were exceptions of course, when the police were seen to be most accommodating. A story has been told about Frederick Lanchester, the car designer and builder, who received the help of a passing constable. After dark, having experienced ignition problems on one of his early designs, Lanchester was able to make adjustments to the engine's running by the light of the bobby's bullseye lantern.

As motor transport became more widely accepted and the means of greater movement than ever before existed, there was more and more need for social change. As criminals used motor cars the police would have to be similarly equipped to catch them. As the population travelled faster and further, so the police were obliged to keep abreast of developments. Probably the first recorded occasion when a motor car was employed to apprehend a criminal was 15 August 1900 at Moor Edge, Newcastle upon Tyne. A horse-rider who was drunk and causing havoc was chased and arrested by a constable who had commandeered a Gladiator Voiturette belonging to an F.R. Goodwin. Subsequently, a number of incidents were recorded where private cars were commandeered for police duty. The incident at Moor Edge demonstrates the arresting constable's initiative, especially at a time when motor cars were seen as suspicious. This incident did much to boost their reputation. The Gladiator in question was hardly representative of its name, the French machine was particularly petite and lacked power, but the event clearly illustrates the motor car's performance and manoeuvrability, compared with either the bicycle or horse.

Some constabularies kept a register of car owners who were willing to make their vehicles available in emergencies, thus eliminating the need for a police force to employ its own vehicles. Such instances where private vehicles were used by the police were not infrequent. The effort involved in commandeering a car, especially at short notice, hardly bears thinking about. Not only were communications infinitely less reliable than they are now, the process of getting a car mobile would have been somewhat protracted. Even as late as 1914, the modes of transport some constabularies had available were archaic. For example, Southend-on-Sea County Borough Constabulary did not have a single motor car, its mechanized transport comprising only three petrol-powered bicycles and two horses. In Lancashire motorcycles were favoured by some forces because they were more manoeuvrable and compared with motor cars, easier to maintain and relatively inexpensive to buy and run. Therefore, apart from a number of motorcycles, the most common means of police transport was the ubiquitous 'bobby's' bicycle; it was customary for constables to purchase their own cycles, for which they received a weekly reimbursement of 2s 6d to include maintenance. Not all constabularies took kindly to bobbies using pedal cycles however. When the Chief Constable of Norfolk wanted to introduce cycle patrols his request was turned down by the County Police Joint Standing Committee, which decreed that bicycles should only be hired in emergencies.

The usefulness of motor cars did not totally go unnoticed by the police, especially those chief constables and senior officers who foresaw their versatility and flexibility of operation. However, the motor car was seen more as a means of administration than of maintaining law and order. There was an immediate problem of maintenance, as police personnel were expert in the care of horses, carriages and bicycles, but new skills would have to be acquired to deal with the petrol engine.

The Metropolitan Police were the first force to sanction the use of a motor vehicle when it experimented with a Léon Bollée petrol-engined tandem three-wheeler at the end of the nineteenth century. Of French origin, Léon Bollées were constructed at Le Mans, home of the now famous motor circuit and in Coventry, courtesy of the Harry Lawson empire. Lawson had wanted to monopolize the British car industry and he invested heavily in a number of projects. One involved the Léon Bollée and Lawson paid £20,000 to acquire the English manufacturing rights. This really was the first very small car, the forerunner of the cyclecar. Its inventor, the son of Amédée Bollée, pioneer of steam road vehicles in France, called it a *voiturette*. Today such machines with their tiny 3hp air-cooled, tube-ignition engines would seem rather feeble, but at that time they were remarkable. Prone to skidding in wet weather, noisy, uncomfortable and often temperamental, the Léon Bollées demonstrated a considerable turn of speed in the right conditions. Sadly, little is known of the results of the Met's trial with the vehicle, although it does illustrate the impact on society the motor car had, even at this very early date.

However, the Léon Bollée three-wheeler, with its belt-driven single rear wheel, might not have been entirely practical. The occupants sat in tandem and had no protection from the weather, but neither had the bobby on a bicycle or horseback. Despite having a crude drive-train, the machine was nimble and capable of reaching 30mph, a speed which was substantially faster than either of its contemporaries, the more robust Panhard or Benz, could muster. The Bollée in fact had achieved considerable fame in November 1896 by taking the first two places in the very first London to Brighton Run. Starting outside London's Metropole Hotel, it took 3 hours, 44 minutes and 35 seconds for the winning car to reach Brighton's seafront; the second car arrived a fraction over fifteen minutes later. It was over an hour later before the car taking third place arrived, a Panhard Wagonette.

In wet weather handling the Bollée proved precarious and the two constables aboard would have been at the mercy of greasy road surfaces. Steering the car required a certain amount of skill, a small hand wheel being located on the driver's right. Braking was uncertain and was controlled by the gear lever, situated on the driver's left, which in addition to selecting the speeds, operated the clutch. For all its shortcomings, the Léon Bollée attracted wide acclaim and received royal patronage when the Duke of Cambridge tried out an example in the grounds of his home. The Hon C.S. Rolls, one of Britain's foremost racing drivers, was also smitten, even if he did record a catalogue of problems, such as the time it took to start and the effort involved in keeping it going.

Traffic congestion in the major conurbations at the beginning of the twentieth century was a particular problem. Horse-drawn cabs, omnibuses, bicycles, hand-barrows, dog-carts and motorcycles all vied for road space with increasing numbers of motor cars. In 1903 a Royal Commission was established to review the problem and after three years' deliberation it recommended improving traffic regulations to include street betterment, control of street works and costermongers and the removal of traffic obstructions. The accident rate in London alone gave cause for concern, especially when as many as 10,000 incidents a year were being recorded.

In 1907 Scotland Yard embarked upon a programme to replace detectives' horse-drawn cabs with motor vehicles. Four cars of unknown make were initially delivered, all of which proved to be sluggish performers, because their small 2-cylinder engines were no match for the heavy landaulette bodywork. It seems likely that as Scotland Yard, under the auspices of the Public Carriage Office, was responsible for drawing up regulations concerning taxi cabs, these vehicles were based on contemporary taxi cab design. Some of the petrol cabs running in London were renowned for their tardy performance, especially the 2-cylinder Rationals with their puny motors. However, not all motor cars suffered from poor performance. Napiers, Argylls and Lanchesters, among others, were renowned for their speed and motor sport successes. By adopting motor cars for its CID officers, the Met formed a mobile squad of detectives which could proceed quickly to the scene of a murder or incident and, as such, pre-dated the formation of the Flying Squad by more than a decade.

While a few other police forces advocated using motor vehicles, their use was often restricted. Mostly it was impractical to cover large distances and factors such as reliability and petrol availability had to be taken into account. The reliability of some cars was proven beyond doubt, competitive events had illustrated that fact, but machines such as Napiers and Rolls-Royces, acknowledged for their successes in motor sport, including the famous Isle of Man Tourist Trophy races, were hardly likely to have been specified by the police because of their relative expense. Petrol was not as widely available as it is today and originally could only be purchased from a chemist. Neither were there garages: the smithy was the nearest to a motor repairer, but could provide little in the way of expertise concerning a car's running gear. Moreover, in all probability, those police forces that had motor vehicles might only have had a single car, which meant that there would have been many demands on its time.

Essex Police were among those constabularies that favoured motor vehicles for senior officers. The force sanctioned the hire of a Belsize 10/12hp car for the Chief Constable, Captain Showers, at the end of 1909. Captain Showers required the vehicle in order to visit justices at different benches and to pay surprise visits to the more remote police stations. The cost, it was argued, was more economical than travelling by train. Before long two Belsizes, two Fords and an Overland were purchased to replace horses which, it was argued, were too expensive to maintain.

One aspect of police work which is seldom recognized is that for many years, until the establishment of a national ambulance service, the police were often responsible for conveying injured or sick people to hospital. As motoring became more widespread and the numbers of accidents increased, so chief constables began requesting the provision of ambulances to care for motor accident victims. This did not happen in all circumstances though, as some boroughs and county authorities administered ambulances independently. The fire service too, in some circumstances, came under police control, thus making policing so diverse that a strain existed on resources generally. In Oldham, for example, the fire service was controlled by the police until 1948, when this responsibility was transferred to county boroughs and ultimately to Lancashire County Council.

The Daimler chassis was often specified for ambulance work and was favoured by Birmingham's police force, among others. Daimlers were at the forefront of design and having been honoured with the Royal Warrant, were used by the Royal Household. Daimler chassis were therefore of the highest repute and infinitely adaptable; when fitted with coachwork designed for ambulance work, the vehicles provided exemplary service. A Daimler saloon was the first car to be used by police in Bolton before the First World War and it is a tribute to the vehicle itself, as well as those who drove and maintained it, that it is still in existence. Now owned by Derek Christian, the Daimler is used as a wedding hire car. Also in Bolton it is recorded that Superintendent James Wilson owned an unnamed car which he used for police work that was driven by a young constable, PC Woodhead.

Until the First World War the majority of police forces in Britain remained largely pedestrian. The Lancashire force, having paid a cycle allowance from 1903, supplied its officers with official bicycles in 1908; probably to do so was more economical. The force introduced a Mounted Police Troop in 1911 and although horses had been used before, they were usually hired from local stables.

Motor cars were fairly slow to evolve at this time, compared with post-war years and many of the designs from 1912 to 1914 shared a number of characteristics with older machines. Even during the latter part of the period cars were still the domain of the aristocracy and the wealthy; chauffeurs were employed and there were few owner drivers. Those motorists who were determined to speed were at the mercy of the speed traps, but of course the police, unlike today, were ill-equipped to give chase.

There is evidence that by 1914 a number of chief constables were using cars. The Chief Constable of Devon was provided with one in 1913 and a constable was appointed as chauffeur, the driving tuition fees costing £5 10s. Kent police had two vehicles by 1914, the Deputy and Chief Constable having individually purchased their cars for which they received an allowance, which reflected both the investment and running costs. Kent, incidentally, had a high proportion of pioneering motorists living in the county and road safety was an issue discussed in schools as early as 1906. In Lancashire, the superintendents had cars in 1918; though this was not so much by design, but because the war had made it difficult to travel around the constabulary by public transport.

Another aspect of police work that is often overlooked is that prior to the First World War few officers would have been able to drive, as their social backgrounds would have prevented them from acquiring such skills. Police forces would have been unable to provide driving tuition from within the ranks and were, therefore, mostly reliant on others to provide this service, usually at a cost. Change though, was around the corner: the war was to determine a new direction.

The First World War was responsible for many changes in social attitudes, and for the first time in a major conflict the motor vehicle saw active service. People who otherwise would not have driven did so and in the case of Birmingham a force of Special Constables, who were enrolled to supplement numbers of police officers called up for military service, formed a volunteer Motor Transport service. The fleet of vehicles, numbering around 100, available to the City of Birmingham Police all belonged to the Specials and in the event of an emergency it was estimated that between 700 and 800 men could be mobilized within an hour.

Policing before the arrival of motor cars meant that bobbies either had to walk their beat, travel by horse or, as depicted here, rely on bicycles. Often officers were required to purchase their own machines and maintain them, for which they received a small allowance. (*Greater Manchester Police Museum*)

The VAUXHALL MOTORIST

Price Four
Vol. 2.
March:

Many Happy Returns!

Motor cars were looked upon as enemies of society and until the repeal of the Red Flag Act in 1896 a speed limit of 4mph was imposed. The few cars that plied British roads were required to be escorted by three persons, one walking twenty yards ahead of the vehicle bearing a red flag. Drivers who exceeded the speed limit were known as 'scorchers' and were at the mercy of the police. In later years the police used various methods to catch speeding motorists, one being to time a car with a stop-watch between two points. This charming caricature which graced the cover of *The Vauxhall Motorist* captures the sense of antagonism that existed between motorists and police. (*Vauxhall Motors*)

A fine body of men! Despite constabularies taking a keen interest in motor cars from the very beginning of the auto industry, they were slow to use such machines for day to day police work. Bitter battles were often fought by motorists, who considered their pleasures were being curbed, and police, who were instrumental in maintaining law and order. (*Greater Manchester Police Museum*)

Beyond doubt the first car used by the police was the Léon Bollée, a French machine, which was powered by a 3hp air-cooled engine with tube ignition. The vehicle won much success in the very first London to Brighton Run in 1896. An example is depicted here with two Metropolitan Police constables. Although undated, the scene can be presumed to be representative of the turn of the century. The Bollées were not noted for their handling and in wet conditions they could be precarious. Steering was effected via a small hand wheel on the driver's right and gears were operated by the lever shown to the left, which also applied the brake. (*Metropolitan Police Museum*)

This collection of vehicles, most of which date from before the First World War, were operated by the Metropolitan Police at Brixton in south London. It is evident that some of the vehicles were used for wartime patrols, as the car on the extreme left bears the All Clear sign. (*Metropolitan Police Museum*)

his Daimler was the first car to be used by Bolton Police and was in service before the First World War. Happily, he car has survived. (*Greater Manchester Police Museum*)

Before the First World War detectives and senior officers within the Metropolitan Police were using cars which were mostly slow and underpowered. After the war the practice continued, but it was cars such as the Model T Ford, as illustrated here, that were used. Two different examples are pictured, each in a different location, along with a detective and his chauffeur. Both cars date from 1918; LT 7769 appears to be outside a police station. Note that the photograph is signed by A. Parker. LT 7776 is seen in a suburban street, possibly in the Brixton area. Not all constabularies used cars. In an emergency they called upon motorists to assist with police operations. (*Metropolitan Police Museum*)

2

Changing Times

The British motor industry emerged from the First World War with unprecedented optimism. Motor vehicles had gone into battle as fighting units, ambulances and fire tenders; as armoured cars they excelled. The family motor car was no longer considered the preserve of the wealthy and professional classes and, consequently, post-war motor shows were over-subscribed with more exhibitors than space.

Changing social conditions meant that even before the end of the war some senior police officers accepted there was a need for the service to be more mobile. While some detectives had regularly used cars, front line officers were often abysmally ill equipped when a quick response was required. In fact, it is recorded that there were only two motor vehicles attached to the Metropolitan Police, both being 10hp Wolseleys fitted with six-seater wagonette bodies. Despite opposition from some chief constables who considered that motor vehicles and indeed almost any type of mechanical device, was unable to supersede a single detective, a move towards fully mobilizing the police was made.

On 21 February 1920 *The Autocar* reported that 'London Police are to be provided with motor cars for controlling traffic, the object being to speed up traffic generally, and the confining of slow-moving vehicles to the kerb'. A year later the Met adopted the 11.9hp Bean as a standard vehicle type and took delivery of several cars, following extensive tests which had been conducted over approximately 10,000 miles. Before this, in 1919, the Metropolitan Police had been split into four detective areas and each division had been allocated two Crossley tenders dating from 1912, which had already seen stalwart service with the Royal Flying Corps.

The Crossleys were used for a wide range of duties, not least the breaking up of criminal gangs. They also supported the fire brigade, as London at this time was largely the focal point of the Irish troubles when fires were deliberately started. A department within the Met, which became known as the 'haystack brigade', had the responsibility of tracking down arsonists and it soon became apparent that the ex-military Crossleys were adept at providing effective police support. The idea of a properly organized, rapid response mobile unit began to take shape: this was the beginning of the Flying Squad.

By today's vehicle standards the Crossley tenders were rudimentary. Although powerful, they were heavy and because they had narrow wheels and tyres they were difficult to steer at speed and in wet weather. Nevertheless, they were reliable and under expert control, quite safe. The Crossleys were fitted with van-type bodies for police operations, which accommodated up to a dozen officers, and were unmarked. It was a long time before the criminals realized that the Crossleys were being used for under cover police work: at times the vehicle bodies, often adorned with detachable name plates of fictitious traders and furniture removers, were replaced to preserve their anonymity. Much of the work carried out with the Crossleys involved patient surveillance of the underworld; the information gleaned was fed back to police headquarters in the interest of wider crime prevention. The operation was notably successful and led to some spectacular arrests.

The effectiveness of an efficient mobile unit was wholly appreciated and resulted in the so-called 'Flying Squad' being updated and re-equipped. One of the most influential developments was radio communication, which was first used by British police in 1923. However the use of radio for policing was not entirely new. In Paris an experiment had already been successful when radio vans communicated with a Farman Goliath aeroplane circling above the city. Trials in Britain were conducted using a fixed radio transmitter installed on the roof of Scotland Yard and a Crossley tender equipped with a mobile receiver. The first official and successful use of radio-telegraphy was at Epsom Downs on Derby Day. Greater numbers of motor vehicles were expected to be on the roads than during pre-war years and congestion around that part of Surrey was obviously going to be enormous. Although still in its early development, wireless was considered to be a most useful means of crime prevention and crowd control. Wireless also complemented a newly installed telephone system linking Scotland Yard with its divisional offices.

The wireless experiment was wholly successful, despite there being a huge amount of equipment necessary to complete the trials. Photographs taken at the time show massive aerials, resembling huge iron bedsteads, fastened to the roof of the Crossley and within the vehicle itself there were extensive transmitting and receiving devices. During those formative days VHF speech transmission was still a long way off and messages were transmitted in Morse; had they been intercepted they would have meant little to all but the most ardent eavesdropper. Other forces followed the Met in installing radio. Lancashire first used wireless in 1924, Morse code again being used for transmissions. A year later the force inaugurated its first mobile wireless unit when a van was equipped with radio during a royal visit to the county.

By the mid-1920s the Met's Crossleys were condemned as outmoded. Criminals had come to recognize the tenders regardless of careful camouflage and the vehicles' speed and performance was no match for more modern types. The Met looked to Coventry, then seen as the home of the British motor industry, for an appropriate sports car for police use. In addition to being fast, the chosen vehicle would have to have earned a reputation for safety and reliability. Not only were vehicles continually improving in performance, but criminals were using fast cars to further their misplaced business. The police, therefore, had to be capable of matching and outstripping even the most powerful cars available, including some American types.

This was a time of rapidly advancing technology: W.O. Bentley was building his 3-litre models which were gloriously snatching records at Brooklands and there were ACs, Rileys, Lagondas, Singers and Sunbeams, to name a few.

It was to Lea-Francis that the police went shopping. An old-established company well known for its bicycles, motorcycles and reliably engineered family cars, Lea-Francis was not particularly recognized for its sporting machines until the arrival of the Hyper in the mid-1920s. The Met, under the direction of Maj T.H. Vitty, bought six 14hp convertibles, each being painted a different colour and without any outwardly visible police markings. Driving Crossley tenders was one thing, but handling a potent sports car, capable of 75mph, was quite another, so the Met embarked on a programme of intensive driver training. Maj Vitty consulted the Flying Squad's most experienced driver, George 'Jack' Frost and the 'Leafs', as they were known, were delivered in May 1927.

The same officers recruited to drive the Crossleys were selected to drive the Leafs. A familiarization process was conducted over several days at Brooklands and the race track was put at the police's disposal, while circuit officials assisted with time measurements, skid tests and road surface trials in order to examine tyre adhesion. Day after day in all weathers, Jack Frost and his fellow Flying Squad officers pushed themselves and their cars to the limit on Brooklands' sharply banked track.

Normally such cars as the Leafs would have been driven with their hoods lowered to afford the least wind resistance and optimum performance. Police operations, however, dictated having hoods raised at all times in the interest of security and covertness on public roads as well as to veil on-board radio equipment, as the aerial was concealed within the hood itself. The Brooklands trials lasted for about a week, after which the Leafs were passed for Flying Squad duties. Flying Squad drivers were renowned for their skills and could handle cars at high speeds with utmost safety under the most difficult conditions. Lea-Francis cars were chosen to spearhead the Flying Squad fleet because of their performance potential and relative light weight. Chassis strengthening was considered, but ultimately this was abandoned so as not to compromize their design and overall performance. The Met was not the only force to favour high performance cars. A number of other constabularies followed London's lead and used sports cars for Flying Squad work which determined the use of specialized vehicles. Only the best were good enough and for a time, in compliance with orders to crack serious crime, senior officers got everything they wanted.

The Met's Leafs worked hard and amassed huge mileages. After two years' exemplary service the cars' engines were showing signs of wear and it was recommended, following consultation with drivers, that the vehicles be replaced. The Leafs' successors would need to be both powerful and reliable, as well as being capable of withstanding some pretty violent use, especially if the only way to stop a bandit car was to ram it. While the Leafs had performed flawlessly, their drivers were nevertheless concerned about the cars' lightness which could be a handicap in the event of a collision. Smash and grab raiders used heavy and powerful cars often fitted with tow bars and would not have thought twice about ramming a police vehicle in order to avoid arrest. Captain (later Sir) Noel Macklin, the highly respected motor engineer and racing driver, was consulted about the choice of vehicle and he suggested Scotland Yard consider the Invicta.

Captain Macklin had recommended the Invicta for no other reason than that it was an excellent machine. Built to a quality associated with the finest of British cars, it benefited by having an engine of great flexibility, a characteristic of some American models of the time. The Invicta was the brainchild of Macklin himself, a venerable figure in the automotive world. His cars were engineered to exceptionally high standards and were regarded as comparable to Bentley and Lagonda. The car Macklin supplied to the Met was none other than the one which had successfully raced at Le Mans.

Major Vitty arranged for Jack Frost to fully evaluate the Invicta at Brooklands. The track was near to The Fairmile at Cobham, Macklin's home and workshop and Invicta engineers were conveniently on hand to provide whatever assistance was necessary. Satisfied with the car's performance under track conditions, Frost put the machine through its paces on the open road, which meant the local police closing the immediate area to all traffic for security and safety reasons. Again the Invicta performed to Frost's complete satisfaction: this was the all-important test after which the car was given the 'thumbs up' and purchased. The Met pioneered the use of Invictas and other forces subsequently specified the marque when fast, reliable and powerful cars were needed. Other models noted for their fine performance were also sought and before long the Met's Flying Squad had a fleet of cars as diverse as Railtons, Lagondas and Bentleys.

Before the Invicta was commissioned several technical modifications were made while the car was at the Met's Chelsea garage. Trials were undertaken along the Thames Embankment, the road being temporarily closed on each occasion in the interests of secrecy; carburettor settings were altered, the engine finely tuned and different sparking plugs fitted. Various components, in compliance with high speed police work, were tried out and when the car went into service it quickly acquired a fine reputation.

Motor cars, by then widely accepted as a necessity rather than a luxury, were being recruited at all levels of police work. Kent Police specified a fleet of Ford Model Ts – affectionately known as Tin Lizzies – for superintendents in 1923 and elsewhere these rugged machines found favour with different forces. Speeding motorists had become a serious problem throughout the country, not least in South Wales where Glamorgan Police were ordered to make great efforts to catch offending drivers. Records indicate that the Glamorgan force was involved in some spectacular chases, but there is no mention of what vehicles were used. Where the Met led, other forces followed. Brighton, for example, was among those forces which also adopted the Lea Francis for Flying Squad work. The General Strike of 1926 had stretched the resources of the Met to the limit and the fleet of only 202 vehicles was viewed as a severe handicap. In addition to the Crossley tenders, of which there were fifty-two, six Austin saloons were reserved for use by the Commissioner and his assistants; thirty-one Bean saloons were complemented by twenty-eight Bean vans; there were eighteen prison vans, one a Dennis, the rest Tilling Stevens. The remainder comprised forty-one Triumph solo and motorcycle sidecar outfits, twenty-four Chater Lea sidecars, and two Austin ambulances. Flying Squad apart, the Met had few trained drivers and any officer with a licence was pressed into driving. Special constables who had cars of their own were expected to loan them for police work and in addition, both AA and RAC patrolmen were enlisted for police duties throughout the duration of the strike.

At around the same time as the General Strike a purpose-built garage and vehicle pool was opened at Lambeth in south London. Subsequently, nearly all motorcycles and combinations were replaced by 7hp 2-cylinder Jowetts which were mainly engaged on administrative work. The decision to purchase lower powered vehicles was one of cost effectiveness. The remaining Crossleys, which had not been designated for Flying Squad duties, were replaced by 14hp Bean vans. Some 12hp Bean tourers were also purchased, but by 1929 these were deemed obsolete and replaced by a variety of vehicles, including 13hp Hillman tourers.

The introduction of police telephone boxes in 1928 brought about a significant development in policing. The once familiar blue boxes were in effect police stations in miniature which afforded a much wider profile of policing than had previously been experienced. Usually installed between half a mile and three-quarters of a mile apart in urban areas, the boxes enabled patrolling bobbies to communicate quickly with headquarters. They were also designed for public use to summon help in the event of an emergency; in schools children were instructed on their use. Police motor patrol crews were therefore able to maintain effective communications even before radio cars were introduced and it was claimed that help could usually be summoned within seven minutes. The value of police boxes was quickly appreciated when, shortly after their introduction, a pedestrian witnessed thieves stealing a car; following a call to the police station from a nearby box, a police chase ensued and the culprits were apprehended.

During the early 1930s vehicles were equipped with two-way radios. This followed an announcement by the Home Secretary who was concerned that the huge number of vehicles on Britain's roads, by then 2.2 million, was responsible for an alarming accident rate. Something had to be done to reduce the number of road fatalities, which by then had reached around 6,500 a year. Before 1930 motor patrols were not entirely favoured in Britain and there was doubt whether they could be operated efficiently. However, America had shown them to be highly successful, and the Met began conducting trials in January 1931, using a Morris car which had been specially adapted for the purpose. Manchester forces followed suit in 1932 after a successful demonstration in Stockport and by September that year Bradford was having spectacular results with radio cars. The radio equipment was bulky and required a third officer, the wireless operator, who was seated in the rear compartment, equipped with headphones and log book. In his autobiography, Jack Frost says that early radio equipment was as powerful as that which was installed in RAF bombers. Two-way radio was used effectively during the 1936 Grand National at Aintree when a Cierra autogyro transmitted traffic information to police cars for efficient crowd and traffic control.

Implementing radio patrols was expensive. During the year ending 31 March 1931 the Met spent over £80,000 on refurbishing its vehicle fleet. Recognizing the huge expenditure to which police forces were committed, the Home Office arranged for constabularies to claim a refund from the road fund grant per operative vehicle. The reimbursement, £120 per annum for a motor car under 12hp and £150 for those above 12hp, was calculated to cover the cost of purchasing, equipping and maintaining vehicles as well as an agreed annual mileage of 13,000. To qualify for a refund, vehicles had to be employed on duties associated with 'supervision of traffic and the prevention and detection of offences in connection with the driving of motor vehicles'. Every vehicle was issued with a log book and the amount of refund was adjusted according to a vehicle's total yearly mileage. For every 1,000 miles above 13,000, between £2 and £5 was added to the reimbursement and for every 1,000 miles below 13,000, between £5 and £12 was deducted. By the end of 1930 there were 950 patrol vehicles nationally, 125 of which were used by the Met.

Manchester established its own Flying Squad in 1930. Some of the force's existing vehicles were replaced by sports cars that were easily capable of speeds in excess of 70mph and in particular a fleet of Alvis cars, including at least one Silver Eagle tourer, which proved highly satisfactory. Alvis, one of the foremost British marques, was established in 1920 and was a force to be reckoned with in terms of motor cars, aero engines and military vehicles. Universally respected for their longevity and performance, Alvis was an obvious choice for high speed police work. In 1931 Armstrong Siddeleys featured strongly in Lancashire's Traffic Department, an organization with considerable influence. After two years and with many thousands of miles recorded, the Siddeleys were retired, having been superseded by six MGs which were purchased for £1,000.

Before 1930 many police forces also used Renaults, Morrises, Humbers, Siddeleys and Fords, including the ubiquitous Model T. Essex police ordered four Model Ts in 1917, for less than £300, and the following year another two more were purchased, as well as two second-hand Belsize cars and an Overland. The Met had at least one Fiat armoured car, which was used when the Commissioner and senior officers visited Ireland and MGs were favoured by many constabularies for fast patrol or Flying Squad work. In London BSA three-wheelers and Morris Cowleys became an increasingly familiar sight and were used for Traffic duties. Oxford City Police were among the first of the provincial forces to use motor cars to strengthen fleets of motorcycles and motorcycle combinations; Morris cars were initially acquired, then MG Midgets. It is hardly surprising that Oxford City Police mostly used Morris and MG cars, as Cowley and Abingdon were close by. Many years later, with the establishment of BMC, the tradition remained.

After 1930 and with motor patrols a familiar sight on British roads, the types of vehicle used by police became all the more diverse. Some constabularies favoured motorcycles, but eventually cars were preferred as they were easier to handle and the law required the corroboration of a second officer when dealing with speeding motorists. Also, many man hours were lost because of poor weather and motorcycle accidents, which led to a reduction of volunteer riders.

Chief Constables were responsible for choosing vehicle types. Until the Second World War the makes employed varied greatly. One of the more unusual was the BSA three-wheeler. Overshadowed to an extent by Morgan, the 'Beeza' three-wheelers differed radically as they had front wheel drive. Based on a Hotchkiss overhead valve 1100cc v-twin water-cooled engine, designed in 1921 to power the BSA Ten, they were driven by a 1-litre derivative of the same motor, BSA having bought the engine manufacturing rights after Morris had acquired Hotchkiss in 1924. BSAs were remarkably successful in motor sport trials events, despite their diminutive size, which is one reason why they were approved for police use. Introduced at the 1929 Motor

Cycle Show, the little BSA proved to be quite innovative. In addition to front wheel drive, it had double transverse leaf-spring independent front suspension coupled brakes – those at the front being inboard – and full electrics. For 1933 a four-cylinder water-cooled engine afforded even greater refinement. The little BSAs had cramped accommodation at the best of times and especially when two burly policemen were on board. Anyone who has driven a BSA three-wheeler will appreciate the awkwardness of changing gear, as the lever is positioned between the driver's legs.

At a time when more and more police vehicles were being introduced, driver training was continually examined and revised. The lack of any proper training facilities had prompted the Metropolitan Police Commissioner to introduce driver training on an established basis and appointed racing driver Sir Malcolm Campbell to test personnel from various departments before preparing a report. Sir Malcolm conducted tests during the late summer of 1934 and recommended that an appropriately equipped driving school was needed. The report said that while it admitted that there was room for some improvement, Flying Squad drivers were highly praised for their skills.

The Metropolitan Police Motor Driving School at Hendon was opened on 7 January 1935 under the supervision of Lord Cottenham, a well-known and highly respected motoring personality. Initially, only single level driver training was offered, courtesy of an inspector, six PCs, a senior civilian instructor and twelve other civilian instructors. Hendon's fleet of cars comprised six 15.9hp and twelve 10hp Hillman tourers. Advanced driving tuition was introduced in January 1936 in order to train Flying Squad drivers properly. Some powerful machines were acquired, including an Alvis Speed 25, a Chevrolet, a Lagonda 4½-litre and a 4½-litre Bentley. By 1937 the Hillmans needed replacing, as many had covered in excess of 110,000 miles. A fleet of Wolseley 14/56hp tourers were purchased, and as these performed exceedingly well they were adopted throughout the entire Met force. The Wolseleys, both tourers and saloons, were adopted by several other forces and for many years they were synonymous with the police car.

In 1937 the Home Office announced that a year-long Experimental Motor Patrol Scheme was to be established in the north-west of England in Cheshire, Lancashire, Liverpool, Manchester and Salford. Additionally, the scheme was extended to Essex and the Met. An intrinsic part of the scheme, as far as the north-west of England was concerned, was the provision of a driving school at Hutton Hall, near Preston, where officers from different forces could be trained. The driving school was set up by Lord Cottenham, who by then was overseeing police driver training throughout the United Kingdom.

Hutton Hall became a centre of excellence; its driver training facilities were impressive and included a skid pan. Lord Cottenham presented the school with a Lagonda which was to be used for skid pan training, but the Chief Constable, A.F. Hordern, decided the car was far too valuable a piece of machinery to be used for such purposes. For many years the Lagonda was used for advanced driver training and today the car is preserved at Hutton Hall in its former glory and is reserved, along with a vintage Bentley, for special duties.

The Experimental Motor Patrol Scheme was essentially a public relations exercise aimed at improving motorists' driving standards and reducing accidents. The scheme was also directed towards improving relations between police and public. During the seventeen months in which it operated, the scheme was an unqualified success. Participating officers were duly dubbed 'Courtesy Cops' by the media; not only were the numbers of accidents substantially reduced, but the Home Office provided 300 personnel and 142 vehicles to enable the scheme to operate efficiently. Proper driver training was adopted by other forces, although in Birmingham, for example, dedicated driver training establishments did not open until after the Second World War.

Throughout the 1930s police cars became an increasingly familiar sight on British roads, as more and more forces dispensed with their two-wheeled transport. However, not all constabularies were convinced by claims that there were substantial economic savings to be had by making motorcycles redundant. Lancashire increased its motorcycle patrol numbers to complement its fleet of motor patrols on the busy Preston to Blackpool Road and speeding motorists soon discovered, to their cost, that there was a patrol for each two miles of road.

West Sussex Police were the first force to fit searchlights to their cars. Bolton Police experimented with SSII tourers, which were forerunners to the Jaguar marque. In Birmingham the twelve 7hp Austin Ruby saloons, costing £1,242, which had replaced a fleet of BSA sidecar outfits between 1935 and 1937, were themselves superseded in 1938 by twenty-six 10hp Austin saloons, fourteen of which were of the fixed head variety that cost £1,544. Essex added two stylish Triumph Dolomite saloons to their fleet in 1938, on top of a number of fabric roofed Hillman Hawk Traffic cars, which had been supplied in 1936. The fabric roofs, incidentally, improved radio reception.

Various forces specified MGs, and the Met had a MkVI tourer for the Flying Squad. Both the Met and the Edinburgh force used MG Midgets, as did Lancashire in 1933 and the East Riding of Yorkshire. Some constabularies ordered the high performance SA and WA saloons, both of which were formidable performers.

Speed restrictions and an increasing use of plain-clothed police patrols were hotly debated in motoring journals during the 1930s. Reports on the enforcement of speed limits were discussed at regular intervals and in March 1935 the subject was raised in Parliament. It was claimed that patrol cars were instructed to cruise at 30mph and any overtaking vehicle was thus considered to be exceeding the speed limit and could be stopped. Members of Parliament were besieged with complaints. Not only had police cars been unmarked, but officers, some female, were operating in plain clothes.

In March 1933 *Commercial Motor* revealed that in some areas of the country mobile police often removed their helmets when on duty and thereby helped to conceal the identity of the police vehicle.

A Home Office spokesman in a Parliamentary reply stated that it was a chief constable's responsibility as to whether unmarked cars with plain-clothed crew were deployed. On a related issue it was decided that police cars, fire tenders and ambulances were exempt speed restrictions when answering emergency calls.

In London the numbers of motor patrols increased from 522 in 1933 to 680 in 1937. The Met's fleet was by now widely varied and included Hillman Wizards, Ford V8-18 Tudors and the small bore Model B, known perhaps inappropriately as the BF. In 1936 London's motor police were responsible for over 140,000 prosecutions, and in excess of 121,000 convictions.

The Flying Squad was established in 1918 in an effort to crack serious crime. Among the vehicles available to the squad were Crossley tenders. Four are shown here at the 1923 Epsom Derby when they were equipped with wireless. The trials proved wholly successful, and thereafter wireless was fitted to Flying Squad vehicles enabling officers to communicate with Scotland Yard. Note the large bedstead-type aerials. (*Metropolitan Police Museum*)

The Met made extensive use of motor cars after the First World War and in 1926 operated a fleet of 202 vehicles. In 1926 a number of 2-cylinder Jowetts were purchased from Ewins' Garage at Banbury, Oxfordshire, mainly for administrative use, including the Public Carriage Office. Ewins' Motor Agents sold various makes of car including Crossley, Wolseley and Ford as well as Jowett. (*Metropolitan Police Museum*)

Anyone who has driven a BSA three-wheeler will know that the cockpit is somewhat confined and there would not have been much space for two burly police officers. The gear change lever on these cars was awkwardly positioned immediately in front of the driver's seat. (*Metropolitan Police Museum*)

A number of BSA three-wheelers were used for Traffic patrol duties in London during the early 1930s. The cars were relatively inexpensive and while they might have appeared unsuitable for police work, they, nevertheless, were successful in motor sport events. This photograph may have been used for publicity purposes, hence the distorted background. (*Metropolitan Police Museum*)

For a short period BSA three-wheelers were a familiar sight on London's streets. GK 6873 is seen emerging from a police yard, the driver wearing white sleeve bands, denoting the car is on Traffic patrol. (*Metropolitan Police Museum*)

The Flying Squad, having moved to cars from Crossley tenders, progressed to such machines as Lea Francis and Invicta, the latter being illustrated here. Racing driver Captain Noel Macklin (later Sir Noel) made an Invicta available to the Flying Squad for evaluation purposes which was eventually purchased. Invictas had a formidable turn of speed which surprised many a bandit! (*Metropolitan Police Museum*)

Morris Cowleys formed a substantial part of the Met's fleet in the early 1930s, many being used for Traffic patrol work. Alongside the car is a BSA 9.86hp motorcycle combination and to the far left of the picture a solo BSA. (*Metropolitan Police Museum*)

Another Morris Cowley 11.9hp tourer, but this time pictured with two BSA 9.86hp motorcycle combinations. Traffic Patrol officers wore flat caps and white wrist bands. (*Metropolitan Police Museum*)

These Austins, pictured *c.* 1929, were used for special duties and were reserved for use by senior officers. (*Metropolitan Police Museum*)

MGs were used throughout the country. Their turn of speed made them ideal for Traffic patrol work. (*Metropolitan Police Museum*)

Bentleys were also used by the Flying Squad, their sporting performance making them highly suitable for police work. Despite this particular car having a Metropolitan Police sign attached to the windscreen, many Flying Squad vehicles were unmarked. This 4½-litre tourer has a Mayfair body and is one of a number of similar vehicles purchased by the Met. (*Metropolitan Police Museum*)

Many a Flying Squad driver would have jumped at the chance to take the wheel of a Bentley, especially this 4½-litre model. Little is known about this car, including the chassis number, other than it was first registered in June 1930. Note the twin sidemounts and the centre lamp. Unfortunately, none of the crew, who look as if they mean business, are identified. (*Metropolitan Police Museum*)

This 4½-litre Bentley (chassis number FB3305) was first registered in 1929, but it was not purchased by the Met until 1938 when it was used by the Flying Squad. The car originally had coachwork by H.J. Mulliner, but has since been fitted with a touring saloon body by Robinson. The car has survived and is presently owned by C. Godwin. (*Metropolitan Police Museum*)

Bean saloons and vans were used by the Met, many being appointed to Barnes garage. Here Superintendent Hawkins is pictured alongside a Bean in 1928 when the car was attached to CID duties. (*Metropolitan Police Museum*)

Croydon Traffic Unit, *c.* 1930. Apart from the BSA three-wheeler (GK 6871), all cars are Morris Cowleys, and th
solo motorcycle is a BSA. Only when the cars are grouped together is the diminutive size of the BSA thre
wheeler appreciated. (*Metropolitan Police Museum*)

Police telephone boxes were introduced in 1928 and, in effect, were police stations in miniature. In urban areas the
were usually situated between half and three quarters of a mile apart. A Fordson police van has answered a ca
from a member of the general public who may have witnessed something suspicious. (*Metropolitan Police Museum*)

he use of radio was viewed with scepticism by some police officers. It was only when criminals were
prehended through its use that its benefits were fully appreciated. Communications is one of many aspects of
licing to have made huge advances over the decades. By comparison to the scenario depicted here, today's
lice vehicles bristle with innovation. Modern technology makes extensive use of satellites, something that these
ficers would possibly have believed to have been of the realms of science fiction.

By the mid-1930s many police cars were fitted with two-way radio equipment and this photograph ably depicts
at such cars required a radio operator as well as an observer. The 100 watt power transmitter was installed in
e boot and remotely controlled by the radio operator sitting in the rear near side seat. The Morse key and
ceiver were fitted within a panel at the operator's side; the aerial, which consisted of strands of insulated wire,
as concealed in the car's roof. (*Metropolitan Police Museum*)

A Flying Squad was established in Manchester in 1930 and it operated on a similar basis to the one in London. Alvis Silver Eagle tourers were used along with BSA motorcycles and motorcycle combinations as support vehicles. Note the familiar blue police box which is situated on Ardwick Green South. These photographs show an Alvis being used as an unmarked car with plain clothes officers sitting in the rear. (*Greater Manchester Police Museum*)

Manchester City Police operated BSA motorcycle combinations; no. 22 is illustrated. Pictured on Ardwick Green South next to one of Manchester's many blue police boxes, this BSA was one of several machines in use. Note the klaxon and the ample leg protectors. (*Greater Manchester Police Museum*)

This Railton was in use with the Met on Flying Squad duties in 1933. Railtons were built in the workshops once occupied by Invicta at Cobham in Surrey, and were the work of Reid Railton who was recognized for his work with World Land Speed Record attempts. The styling of Railtons was not unlike Invictas, although they were built on Terraplane 8 chassis with 4-litre engines. (*Greater Manchester Police Museum*)

A 25hp Wolseley with ambulance body. For many years the Police Service was responsible in some areas for administering ambulances. This Wolseley was used to convey sick and injured policemen to hospital. (*Metropolitan Police Museum*)

One of the more unusual vehicles in police fleets during the inter-war years was this Railton Special Saloon used by the Met in 1938. This is a 21.6hp model, the Hudson 3½-litre engine providing 80mph top speed. (*Metropolitan Police Museum*)

1933 the Met took several Ford Bs into its fleet. The cars were improved Model As and as they were fitted with nall bore engines, they were known rather unfortunately as BFs. Note the police sign in the front window. (*Ietropolitan Police Museum*)

Ford BFs were designed with efficiency in mind. The fuel tank was relocated from beneath the scuttle to the rear of the car and they had 2-litre engines. The bodies were made by Briggs on site at Dagenham. This general purpose car, which was fitted with wireless, has an opening windscreen. (*Metropolitan Police Museum*)

The 'Stop Police' sign on this Ford BF was hand operated from the driving position. It consisted of a pull-type blind suitably inscribed. (*Metropolitan Police Museum*)

Two of the Met's Ford BFs pictured outside Scotland Yard on 25 October 1933. (*Metropolitan Police Museum*)

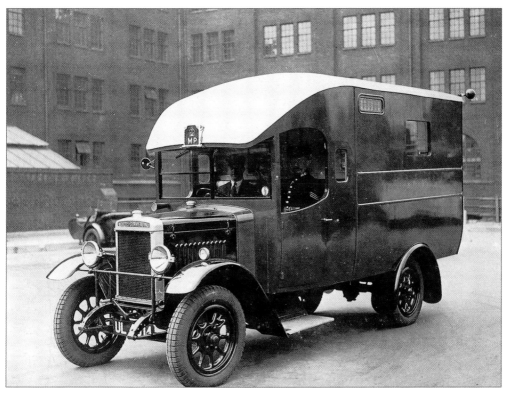

Support vehicles form an essential part of any police fleet. This Morris Commercial van was used at the beginning of the Police Box scheme in 1929 and served mainly in two locations, Richmond (Surrey) and Wood Green (north London). (*Metropolitan Police Museum*)

Prison vans came under police jurisdiction; the Met used this Leyland Cub vehicle in 1938. Some prison vans were dual purpose; the interior could be converted to accommodate police officers or, when required, the carriage of general supplies. (*Metropolitan Police Museum*)

Photographic vans were used by the Met; this Commer was service in 1939. Such vehicles assisted at crime scenes and we fully equipped as a mobile darkroom. (*Metropolitan Police Museum*

A 1936 Commer Utility van which would have been used for general purposes. (*Metropolitan Police Museum*)

A 1938 Commer, also a general purpose vehicle. (*Metropolitan Police Museum*)

The Met purchased a number of Hillman Wizard '65' tourers for Traffic patrol duties; shown here is AGX 627. These cars were fitted with 6-cylinder side valve engines and 4-speed gearboxes without synchromesh. (*Metropolitan Police Museum*)

Another view of AGX 627 with the same crew, this time pictured outside the Hinckly Wood Hotel in south-west London, not far from Hampton Court. (*Metropolitan Police Museum*)

A 16.9hp Hillman Tourer pictured while on Traffic patrol work in 1939. (*Metropolitan Police Museum*)

Accidents do happen . . . but not all incidents are what they seem. On occasions Flying Squad drivers were forced to stop raiders by all means possible, even if it meant ramming a car, or being rammed. Pictured within the confines of Scotland Yard, this Hillman has received substantial damage. (*Metropolitan Police Museum*)

Le Mans-type start? Whatever the occasion these officers seem to be enjoying the event. There are several vehicle types in this picture including Hillman tourers and saloons. The picture was taken in 1934 when driver training was reviewed. The Metropolitan Police Commissioner introduced training for all drivers and appointed Sir Malcolm Campbell to prepare a report on whether the establishment of a driving school was necessary. (*Metropolitan Police Museum*)

Few cars can boast such splendid styling as these Talbot tourers that were in service during 1937 with Norfolk Constabulary. While the cars look as if they might have plenty of power they were no match for some of the large-engined tourers of the era, such as Jaguars, Bentleys and Lagondas. (*Colin Chipperfield Collection*)

The Metropolitan Police on parade. Traffic Patrol officers salute Queen Mary in 1934. The cars are all Hillman Wizard tourers as used by the Met's Traffic Department. (*Metropolitan Police Museum*)

Vauxhalls were used for Traffic patrols as well as Hillmans and other cars. This is a Light Six Saloon which shared some styling similarities with the Big Six, although the engine was set forward in a redesigned frame. Under heavy braking the cars were known to curtsy, the suspension affording an otherwise soft ride in the American manner. (*Metropolitan Police Museum*)

In 1935 the Hillman Wizard made way for the Hillman Hawk, which had an all-new chassis frame and independent front suspension. The bodies were built by Pressed Steel and had much in common with the Humber 12hp. Spacious and relatively powerful, courtesy of Hillman-Humber 6-cylinder engines, these cars were used by a number of constabularies, including the Met, as well as many government departments. (*Metropolitan Police Museum*)

mall horsepower Austins were used by several constabularies, often in connection with administrative work.
he cars were acknowledged for their reliability and quality, it is little wonder the cars sold in large numbers.
After the First World War Austin initially provided only one model, the Twenty, but dwindling sales nearly
ankrupted the company. Two models were introduced, the Twelve and Seven, the former being a scaled-down
ersion of the Twenty; the Seven, introduced in 1922, was Austin's salvation and proved to be one of the most
uccessful motor cars of all time. Other models introduced during the 1930s include the 10/4, Cambridge 10,
scot 12 and the Goodwood 14, all of which were keenly sought by a nation in love with the motor car.

These Austins carry Cornwall registrations from 1938, and presumably were operated by Devon and Cornwall
onstabulary. (*Colin Chipperfield Collection*)

This MG TA Midget used by the Met could well have been on loan from Lancashire Constabulary, as it had a large fleet of these cars, including CTC 686. Note the substantial police signs above the windscreen and at the rear. A profile view of this car is seen on page 55. (*Metropolitan Police Museum*)

Pictured at Lancashire Constabulary's police driving school, these two fine vehicles are used on special occasions. The Bentley (Vanden Plas coachwork) dates from August 1923 (chassis no. 152) and is fitted with low geared steering and four-wheel brakes; the Lagonda was presented to the school by Lord Cottenham, but the Chief Constable considered the vehicle too valuable to be used for skid pan training. Lord Cottenham, who did much to promote road safety, was appointed by the Home Secretary to oversee police driver training throughout the country. Under his supervision Hendon Police Driving School opened in January 1935. (*Author's collection*)

This Alvis tourer was pictured at Hutton Hall, near Preston, soon after the Driving Centre was established in 1937. Recognized for its impressive facilities, Hutton Hall served as a driver training school for many years and was used by a number of constabularies in northern England. (*Greater Manchester Police Musuem*)

This MG VA tourer was one of six cars purchased by West Riding (Yorkshire) Police in 1938. These cars had 1548cc overhead valve engines, as fitted to the Wolseley 12. (*Colin Chipperfield Collection*)

The City of Manchester Police operated this fleet of Wolseleys, similar vehicles having been employed by the Met and other constabularies in order to operate the Experimental Motor Patrol Scheme. The cars provided exemplary service and the marque became synonymous with police work over many years. (*Colin Chipperfield Collection*)

Part of the Met's fleet pictured in 1939. There is an interesting array of cars here, some of which are prepared for blackout operations. As well as Wolseleys there is a 4½-litre Bentley, a Triumph Dolomite, a Talbot, a Humber and a Buick, which gives rise to the belief that these were Flying Squad vehicles. (*Metropolitan Police Museum*)

This 1937–8 Hillman 14hp was pictured in 1939 complete with wartime specification to include offside blackout lamp and white markings to the wing edges, running boards and bumpers. (*Metropolitan Police Museum*)

William Morris acquired Wolseley in 1927 and in 1935 incorporated the company within the Nuffie[...] Organisation together with Morris. Wolseley engines, long acknowledged for their fine engineering, found the[...] way under the bonnets of Morris Minors and MGs. Wolseley chassis continued to be made available to a numbe[...] of bespoke coachbuilders in the late 1930s, this being significant at a time when traditional coachbuilding wa[...] sliding into decline. The famous Wolseley illuminated oval badge was introduced in 1932 and provided th[...] marque with a unique trademark that remained until the cars went out of production in the 1970s.

In addition to saloons, Wolseley tourers were used by the Met for Traffic duties. This particular car is picture[...] in a somewhat serene location in 1939. (*Metropolitan Police Museum*)

3

No Hiding Place

The Second World War brought dramatic consequences for the police, as well as the fire and ambulance services, both of which were often administered by the former. During the second half of the 1930s, when war seemed unavoidable and imminent, the government had funded the building of several Shadow Factories, which were mostly allied to the motor industry and which provided for the war effort by manufacturing aero engines, aircraft assemblies and tanks. Before the end of 1940, when motor vehicle production for civil use was halted, virtually all of Britain's car production plants were converted to producing military materials. So when the Chief Constable of Birmingham attempted to replace his fleet of patrol cars that year, he found it virtually impossible to do so.

Birmingham's patrol cars had clocked up a minimum of 58,000 miles each and in order to keep the fleet in its usual prime condition it was cost effective to replace it rather than to embark upon costly repairs. When he applied to the Home Secretary to sanction the replacement, Birmingham's Chief Constable was firmly rebuked. The entire budget for police cars nationwide extended to no more than twenty-five vehicles in 1940. In Birmingham's case, however, the situation was relieved when, according to *Policing Birmingham* (published by West Midlands Police in 1989), fourteen second-hand cars, some having fewer than 8,000 miles recorded, were acquired.

As in the First World War, many policemen were called up in 1939, thus leaving a shortfall of officers. In many instances, such as Birmingham, the Women's Auxiliary Service provided essential personnel, including drivers.

During the war there was a reduction in the number of police cars used for routine duties, as certain operations were scaled down or even curtailed. Some vehicles were moth-balled while others, to prevent them deteriorating, were used on a rotational basis. Fuel supplies were very limited and therefore the most economical use of petrol was made. Those vehicles that remained in service were subject to black-out conditions, which meant that wing edges were painted white and headlamps were diffused so that only the most minimal light was emitted. This in itself was the cause of many accidents, as drivers had to contend with restricted visibility and vehicles were often unseen by pedestrians at night. Motorcycles were favoured for patrol work, their manoeuvrability being particularly advantageous in the rubble-strewn streets of war-torn cities. Motor car patrols remained to some extent, although during the day these were reduced by around 50 per cent, and largely ceased at night.

Police vehicles fulfilled a diverse range of duties throughout the war, from ensuring that blackout conditions were maintained to instructing how gas masks should be worn in the event of a gas attack, using specially prepared 'gas' vans. Fuel restrictions alone dictated that there were fewer motorists on the road, and therefore traffic accidents and car crime were drastically lower than in peace time. However, often spot checks were made by Traffic Department officers to deter the illegal use of specially coloured petrol, which was made available to essential users.

Bombing raids brought fear and chaos to many of Britain's towns and cities. In addition to the stationary air raid sirens usually installed on public buildings, it was not unusual to see police patrol vehicles fitted with roof-mounted amplifiers touring out of town districts to supplement the warnings. Before the war these patrol cars, with their roof-mounted amplifiers, were used to enhance the government's high profile road safety campaign. It was once commonplace to see the cars positioned at well-known accident black spots or at notorious road junctions. Information about road safety was broadcast to drivers and pedestrians alike. The campaign was often accepted with good humour, but not always, as some people felt humiliated at their wrong-doings, lack of judgment or lapse of concentration being broadcast for all to hear. As citizens rushed to air-raid shelters, so police patrol car crews went about their normal business. They were responsible for arresting many housebreakers and looters who took advantage of temporarily unoccupied homes and shops.

Many significant technical developments had taken place during war time. Possibly the most influential for the police was ultra high frequency radio (UHF). A pilot scheme was tested in Birmingham in August 1942. The introduction of UHF radio had the backing of a strong marketing strategy within the City of Birmingham Police. The force occupied floor space in Lewis' department store in the city centre as a means of publicizing its effectiveness. Before the days of 999 the police actively encouraged the use of an easy-to-remember number – in this instance Central 5000 – for the public to contact the emergency services. In Lewis' Birmingham Police exhibited a patrol car fitted with a UHF radio-telephone and a mock-up of a police control room, complete with police personnel who offered advice and information.

Nowhere was radio used to better effect than in Manchester when, in December 1940, the Divisional Police Headquarters at Old Trafford was destroyed by enemy bombing. It was during that air raid that eight police personnel and an air raid warden were killed. Shortly afterwards the Divisional Headquarters at Seaforth was bombed and during the same attack the regional telephone exchange received a direct hit, which put Liverpool's entire communications network out of action. Lancashire Constabulary went to the rescue; it made available its police wireless cars to provide an emergency radio system, along with a flock of carrier pigeons donated by local fanciers. During the war it is estimated that fanciers supplied approximately 7,000 pigeons nationally to support communications.

The Met was also instrumental in developing radio communications and experimented in a specially prepared room at Scotland Yard with equipment supplied by the Royal Navy. When at least 100 radio cars were to be introduced into the Met's 700 square mile area, Lt Cdr K.B. Best was appointed Force Communications Officer and ultimately, through the Home Office, became Wireless Officer to police forces throughout the country. Regardless of how efficient Birmingham's or the Met's radio operation proved to be, it could not match that of Nottingham which was claimed to be the most modern and reliable of its day.

After the war traffic congestion was largely unknown as petrol rationing continued until 1950. As far as the police were concerned this hiatus afforded some time during which vehicle fleets and future requirements could be appraised; worn out models for which replacements or spare parts could not be obtained were disposed of in readiness for the delivery of new vehicles once the motor industry was fully re-established. Regardless of fuel shortages many motorists recommissioned their cars and those who were in the fortunate position to purchase new vehicles did so, despite the fact that an enforced export drive meant that relatively few cars were actually available for the home market. Nevertheless, the period before the end of petrol rationing was one of increasing road use, which gave rise to a serious escalation in the numbers of accidents and fatalities. With the abolition of rationing the situation was even more acute. The morbid statistics were responsible for the government introducing special patrols within the Traffic Accident Group Scheme of 1947 with the proposal that patrols should be sent to areas of serious traffic congestion or scenes of major accidents. The most economical use of vehicles was sought and in London twenty-four patrols were established. Each comprised a Wolseley, fitted with two-way radio and directional loudspeakers and a pair of Triumph motorcycles. When not attending to major incidents, the crews were expected to concentrate on accident prevention.

The boom in car ownership was largely socially orientated. Peacetime, despite years of austerity, produced an era of financial growth, an expanding population and the establishment of new towns. New and better roads encouraged greater reliance upon private, rather than public, transport, all of which placed demands upon adequate policing.

The Traffic Accident Group Scheme caught full media attention with patrols likened to 'New York Traffic Cops'. Forces outside London adopted similar schemes, the underlying principle being road safety much as in the similar pre-war Experimental Traffic Scheme. Throughout Britain specially trained officers were sent to schools seeking to impress on children the importance of looking and listening before crossing roads, the message being 'look right, look left and look right again before you cross'. School road safety events were designed to impress, and playgrounds were transformed into streets complete with pedestrian crossings and traffic lights. The dangers associated with roads and vehicles were acted out with the full horrors of a road accident and the thrills of seeing police cars in action, complete with the familiar shrill sounding of the gong and the screeching of tyres, became part of the curriculum.

As post-war police fleets were re-equipped it was the chief constables who were among the first to receive new vehicles, Armstrong Siddeley, Hillman Minx, Humber

Hawk, Humber Super Snipe and Wolseley limousines being particularly favoured. Elsewhere an assorted collection of cars were making their appearance, including the sleekly styled Riley 1½-litre RMA/RME and its 2½-litre sister-cars RMB and RMF. Jowett Javelins, with their fast-back styling, flat-four engines and all-torsion bar suspension were also popular in some areas, as well as Railtons and MGs, both of which were often reserved for Flying Squad duties.

MG had specialized in supplying cars adapted for police use and over 400 vehicles were delivered to thirty constabularies before the Second World War. The company served the police well and were always willing to accommodate a force's requirements for equipment and specification. It was customary for MG to modify their engines with specially designed cylinder heads, which increased the capacity of the standard 1½-litre car from 1548cc to 1750cc. High lift camshafts, special conrods and pistons were fitted, all of which produced 63bhp at 5500rpm. In addition to engine modifications, which also called for a modified clutch to cater for extra torque, several special features were incorporated into the cars' equipment specification. Speedometers were guaranteed accurate within the tight parameters that were set, police-approved radios and transmitting devices were fitted, together with necessary aerials, first-aid equipment, megaphones, Dulci public address systems, spotlamps and fire extinguishers.

Sunbeam Talbots were enlisted in some forces as well as the more familiar Vauxhalls, Wolseleys and small horsepower Hillmans. There were some less familiar cars too, including pre-war SS Jaguars and Triumph Dolomites as well as the highly innovative Citroën Six, the immortal Traction Avant, with its monocoque body and low centre of gravity, which in later years became synonymous with the literary Parisian police detective, Maigret. There were some prestigious cars fulfilling unusual roles, such as the post-war 4¼-litre Bentley Standard Steel Mark VI Saloon, and the pre-war Lagonda LG6, which had much W.O. Bentley influence.

Among the cars made available for police work was the Austin A70 Hampshire. A number of forces purchased them, including the City of Birmingham who took fifteen in 1949 together with a Bedford coach. With its bulbous wings (those at the rear were semi-enclosed with detachable panels to facilitate wheel changing), the Hampshire looked like an overgrown Austin A40 Devon. The styling followed the American idiom, which was popular at the time, and there were certain similarities shared with Chevrolets of the early 1940s, albeit in compact form. Powered by a 2.2-litre engine inherited from the Austin Sixteen, the car performed well enough, but was not particularly easy to handle. Hampshires were primarily built for export and had a column-shift gear change which, in this instance, was awkward and difficult in action. The brakes were of the hydro-mechanical variety and because they lacked feel, were not known for their sharp performance. To further dampen the car's appeal, for its overall size it afforded little more accommodation than its smaller, sister car.

Birmingham, like most forces, had resources that were fully stretched, and it was because of this that the constabulary used its fleet of Hampshires to operate a courtesy scheme, whereby motorists were merely cautioned regarding minor law infringements. Only when drivers were stopped for excessive speeding or dangerous driving were proceedings taken.

The rapidly increasing number of vehicles using Britain's roads caused police chiefs to debate, not for the first time, introducing dedicated traffic units. It was claimed that London and provincial cities were virtually at vehicle saturation point, something acknowledged even in the early 1950s and congestion had reached a stage then considered to be out of control. In particular the increase in road traffic was very noticeable in the cotton towns of Lancashire. To police the county the constabulary had 280 cars, comprising a number of Austins, Hillmans, Humbers, Standard Vanguards, Jaguars, Ford Pilots and black MGs. Additionally, sixty-six motorcycles supplemented the fleet.

It was intended that traffic units should enforce parking restrictions and ensure that main thoroughfares and through routes remained clear. The Central Traffic Squad was formed in July 1955. In May 1955 plans for the squad's introduction were well advanced when a seventeen-day rail strike crippled London and the south-east, so it became the ideal time to test the embryonic squad's effectiveness.

Morris Oxfords were the backbone of the Central Traffic Squad fleet and each car was equipped with a radio telephone. Often the need arose for high speed driving, which called for expert handling and control techniques. As Traffic Squad fleets were introduced to large provincial cities, so each force favoured particular vehicles. Among those most preferred was the Wolseley Series III 18/85 with its in-line 6-cylinder 2322cc engine which had its debut in 1938. Post-war production resumed in the autumn of 1945 and in 1948 was replaced by the 6/80, which had many similarities with the Morris Six.

Efficient and effective policing meant that there was need for increasing reliance upon technology and as such gave rise to the use of radar to record a vehicle's speed and on-board cameras to record, when appropriate, examples of dangerous or careless driving as they happened. It was further recognized that police patrol crews should be provided with the necessary equipment to deal with a wide range of incidents, including road traffic accidents, and to warn of hazards at all times.

Speed detection devices were not well received by the motoring public who considered them a hindrance to their motoring enjoyment. It was even more frustrating for drivers having to accept that the readings from radar equipment, the accuracy of which was viewed with huge suspicion, could be used in court to secure a speeding conviction. The use of cameras installed in police cars were viewed with similar mistrust and many drivers, to their cost, discovered how advancing technology was being used to determine a safer environment. Walkie-talkie sets were used by the police for the first time in 1950 when the trapping of speeding motorists by officers of the Wiltshire Constabulary did not go unnoticed by the motoring press. An experimental scheme using walkie-talkies was successfully tried out by officers on horseback in 1936 (the sets were known as 'horse-talkies') when policing the Grand National at Aintree.

The Autocar in February 1950 was moved to publish a stinging editorial chastizing police authorities for wasting time and money, as well as inviting potential danger as drivers concentrated not so much on the road, but avoiding prosecution should they stray slightly above speed limits. Trials using warning portable lamps, signs and other equipment for use in an emergency and to warn other road users of hazards, proved entirely successful. The equipment was so commodious, however, that it was not easily installed in a saloon car, and fleets of Humber estate cars and similar vehicle types were generally employed nationally to provide what is now a familiar and essential service.

In contrast to the kit found on American police cars some twenty years earlier, that carried on British police cars seemed minimal. American kit included a siren, search lamps, compass, heater, ten ton hydraulic jack, fire extinguisher, gas masks and tear bombs, automatic rifle, blanket and stretcher, rope and grappling hook, radio equipment and a camera.

Effective maintenance was essential to the reliability of police vehicles and each force had its own service and repair facilities. These were operated with model efficiency and were inspirational to many commercial garages. While each constabulary had its own operating procedures, the emphasis was on preventive maintenance, thus ensuring vehicles remained in optimum condition. Along with other forces, the Met had clearly defined servicing schedules, so that during the late 1940s and early 1950s all police cars operated two eight-hour shifts before undergoing a mandatory check-over, wash and top-up of oil and fluid levels. Police drivers conducted their own routine maintenance at 500 mile intervals and at 5,000 miles every vehicle was subjected to a complete overhaul and inspection. Most forces had their own breakdown and recovery fleets, which in the case of the Met comprised Scammell mechanical horses and Bedford and Fordson tow trucks. Careful routine maintenance was the key to a fleet's longevity: during the early post-war years the estimated life of a police car was up to 300,000 miles, whereas at one time this was no more than 60,000 miles.

To many people the Wolseleys of the mid-1950s epitomized the classic police car. To some extent this is true although Rileys and MGs from the same period were also nominated for police work, all three marques being derived from the same stable and apart from relatively minor styling differences, were similar in appearance. This was the British Motor Corporation at its best, regarding badge engineering, a theme that continued throughout two decades and more. Most of the differences between the models related to running gear and the appointment of the cars' interiors. The Wolseley 4/44 took over from the 4/50 in 1952, and the 6-cylinder version, the 6/90, was introduced in 1954 to replace the 6/80. Riley introduced the 4-cylinder 2443cc Pathfinder in 1953 and in 1958 the 2.6, which was almost identical to the Wolseley 6/90, apart from wider section tyres, bucket seats and marginally more power. The MG Magnette ZA 1.5-litre arrived in 1953 and was superseded by the Magnette ZB in 1956. Outwardly, the cars were similar, but the ZB had a wrap-around rear window, a slight variance of exterior coach trim and a more powerful version of the ZA's engine, together with a higher ratio rear axle.

Much of the reason for the Wolseley becoming synonymous with police work was that in London and other large cities these cars, or those from the BMC stable, were often used for Traffic patrol and 'Q' car work. More often than not the shrill ringing of a gong would signal a black Wolseley effortlessly responding at high speed to an emergency. The use of Wolseleys, and indeed any type of police car, proved to be an excellent marketing tool for the manufacturer. Complementing the big Wolseleys, Austin A90 6-cylinder Westminsters found some favour, and for police use Austin supplied the cars with laminated windscreens and speedometers that were synchronized for accuracy. Predictably, they were all painted black. Police cars conveyed an image of speed with reliability, and many motorists looked no further than their BMC showroom when ordering a new car.

Wolseleys were and are romantically linked with the television and cinema films depicting policing of the era. *Dixon of Dock Green*, *Dial 999* and *No Hiding Place* were favourites and to a great extent served as propaganda, as well as being highly entertaining. *Dixon of Dock Green* was based on the film *The Blue Lamp*, which was made in cooperation with Scotland Yard and released in 1950. Such programmes alluded to a low crime rate as a result of effective police intelligence, when in fact crime was steadily rising at a time when there was a shortage of police officers.

At the end of the 1950s Wolseleys again featured in police television dramas when the 6-99, and later (in 1961) the 6-110 superseded the 6/90s – note the style change to model designation. This was the period of the Farina-styled cars, the Italian styling connection introduced by BMC to give their cars greater prestige, as well as some keener individuality. These later Wolseleys belong to a different era and are discussed in length later.

Wolseley prepared for wartime use. During the Second World War many of the country's police officers were called up and consequently there was a lack of drivers. Those officers who, for whatever reason, did not go to war were joined by civilians as well as the Women's Auxiliary Service. (*Metropolitan Police Museum*)

Scotland Yard in the late 1940s. The Wolseley 14/60 was introduced in 1938 and used until 1948. The car illustrated carries a 1946 registration, but similar vehicles provided London and provincial police with essential transport throughout the war years. Wolseleys and other cars formed the backbone of the Traffic Accident Group Scheme, when it was established in 1947 in response to growing traffic congestion and a rapidly rising accident rate. (*Metropolitan Police Museum*)

Off the simulator, out of the classroom and taking lessons from a driving instructor in an MG. (*Metropolitan Police Museum*)

A Humber Snipe, *c.* 1946. Note the large mirror fitted to the off-side front wing, an attachment found on most Metropolitan Police cars. The fact that this vehicle is without a bell suggests it was being used by the Flying Squad or as a 'Q' car. (*Metropolitan Police Museum*)

The skid pan at Hutton Hall, Lancashire Constabulary's driver training school. Onlookers may be wondering if the pupil handling the Wolseley will successfully steer around the tyre. . . . (*Greater Manchester Police Museum*)

In post-war years driver training was treated with the same emphasis as pre-war. Here drivers are having their response time tested at Hendon on an early type of simulator. (*Metropolitan Police Museum*)

The Traffic Accident Scheme included teaching children road safety drill, which meant that police officers visi schools. Such events were mostly exciting, especially when police cars scorched around playgrounds a perimeters of playing fields with the ensuing role play. This is obviously a 'planned accident', the driver of Hillman having knocked a cyclist from his machine. Note the Wolseley 14/60 complete with bell and ro mounted loudspeakers. (*Metropolitan Police Museum*)

The Traffic Patrol Scheme was seen by the media to emulate the New York Courtesy Cops. Patrol units comprised a Traffic car with a two-man crew and two solo motorcyclists. One such patrol is seen here in about 1947 giving assistance to a driver on a busy arterial road on a sunny day. Judging by the amount of traffic could this have been a bank holiday? (*Metropolitan Police Museum*)

Traffic patrols in Burnley, *c.* October 1948. The Traffic Patrol Scheme was introduced across the country. As well as attending known accident black spots and areas of congestion, patrols did much to try and improve standards of driving. The cars depicted are all Wolseleys and the motorcycles are BSAs. (*Greater Manchester Police Museum*)

A Humber Snipe area wireless car is responding to a 999 call in London, *c.* 1948. It was fortunate that a police officer was patrolling the vicinity to allow the squad car to proceed. In the background can be seen The Angel Hotel, and on the corner the Fifty Shilling Tailors, a popular men's outfitters where demobbed personnel could buy their 'civvy' suits for the equivalent of £2.50! (*Metropolitan Police Museum*)

West Riding Police used Austin Hampshires; this example dates from about 1949. The handling of these cars, with their hydromechanical brakes and column gear change, could be tricky, but the engines were very reliable. (*Colin Chipperfield Collection*)

Bedford OB buses and coaches were used extensively throughout British police forces to convey squads of officers to football matches and other events. They were also the mainstay of many bus operators, but by the late sixties had become rare. Vehicles such as the one illustrated had simply upholstered seats, while commercial ones were more luxurious. The lower picture shows interior detail. (*Metropolitan Police Museum and Vauxhall Motors*)

A Wolseley 14/60 Traffic Patrol car, escorted by two solo motorcycles, leaves Scotland Yard, *c.* 1950. Judging by the police presence and the officer stopping oncoming traffic, it can be assumed this was a special occasion. (*Metropolitan Police Museum*)

A Vauxhall Motors representative hands over a Bedford OB Black Maria and two Vauxhall cars to the police. Little is known about the occasion, but all vehicles have Middlesbrough registrations which suggests the vehicles were for Middlesbrough Traffic Department. The car on the far left of the picture is a 2275cc Velox, first introduced in 1948, and that on the far right is a new generation 1442cc Wyvern, which became available in 1951, the year this photograph was taken. (*Vauxhall Motors*)

HM The Queen with the Duke of Edinburgh pictured in Hyde Park when she reviewed the police forces of the United Kingdom. Note the specially adapted Land Rover. It did not require a vehicle registration plate because it was being used for State purposes. (*Metropolitan Police Museum*)

Pictured in Manchester, this Morris J-type van was one of many used by constabularies. These vehicles were first shown at the Commercial Motor Show at Earls Court in 1948, but did not go into production until 1949. Originally badged as Morris Commercials, most J-types simply carried the Morris name; in 1957 J-types became JB Express delivery vans. (*Greater Manchester Police Museum*)

Morris Commercial PV vans, such as the type depicted, were a familiar sight around Britain in the early 1950s. Note the front bumper which was fitted 'in-house' by the Metropolitan Police. (*Metropolitan Police Museum*)

The Wolseley 6/80 was successor to the 14/60 and, as such, is for many people the archetypal police car. Th particular example is being used for training purposes at Hendon Driving School while a pupil attempts to revers (*Metropolitan Police Museum*)

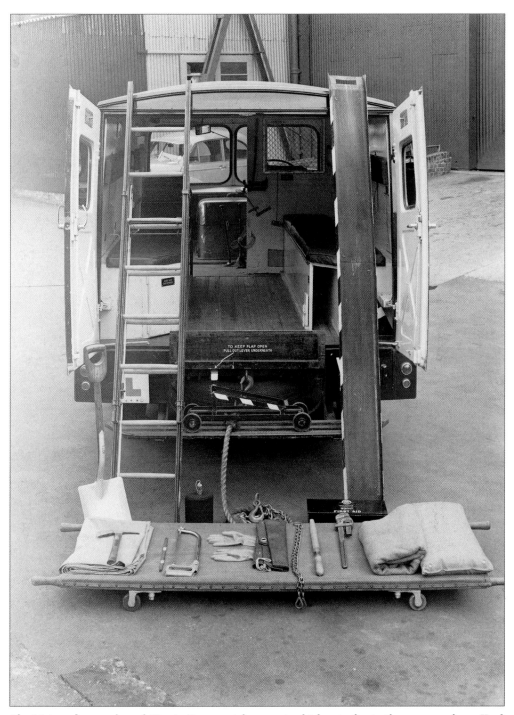

The Met used a number of Morris Commercial support vehicles similar to the one seen here. Used for training purposes – note the 'L' plate – the vehicle's austere furnishings are evident. An early, split screen Morris Minor is just visible through the van's windscreen. (*Metropolitan Police Museum*)

An unusual candidate for police work was the Daimler SP250; this example dates from May 1961. Often known as the Daimler Dart (Daimler dropped the appellation following a complaint from Dodge who already used it), the car had 120mph performance from an engine giving it superb flexibility. There is little wonder that officers almost fought over driving the 2.5-litre sports car. (*Metropolitan Police Museum*)

An unusual assortment of police vehicles pictured outside the Met's Police Driving School. The Daimler SP250s had glassfibre bodies and early models, dating from 1959, tended to suffer from a lot of vibration. The later series of cars, from 1961, had stiffer frames and bodies, and were more reliable. This 1961 picture illustrates a brace of Triumph motorcycles together with two motor scooters. (*Metropolitan Police Museum*)

e Met operated a varied assortment of vehicles, a few of which are shown here. Nearest to the camera is a
kII Jaguar, next to it a Ford Zephyr 6. Further along can be seen an Austin A99/110 Westminster, a Rover
litre, a Vauxhall Cresta/Velox, a Wolseley 6-99/6-110, a Standard Vanguard and another Rover. In the distance
n be seen a Land Rover and an Austin or Morris 1½ ton van. (*Metropolitan Police Museum*)

ncashire Constabulary used a fleet of Ford Zephyrs to police the new towns on Merseyside, the same that were
ed to good effect in the BBC Television series *Z-Cars*. These are Area Traffic cars which were painted black.
otorway patrol vehicles were white and were only driven by officers with an advanced certificate. (*Greater
anchester Police Museum*)

Wolseley 6/90s were frequently seen in London at the end of the 1950s and early 1960s. Synonymous with the Flying Squad, the cars became all the more familiar to film-goers and television viewers who relished such programmes as *Dixon of Dock Green*, *Dial M for Murder* and *No Hiding Place*. The 6/90s were built between 1954 and 1959 and used BMC's six-cylinder 2,639cc C-series engine.

Responding to a 999 call these two Wolseley 6/90s (1959 vintage) along with a 1958 Morris Commercial LD van have arrived at a large department store in London's West End. (*Metropolitan Police Museum*)

Police patrol cars were required to carry ever increasing amounts of equipment, which meant that forces moved to introduce 'incident cars' which could speed to an accident or hazard. The Met used Humber Super Snipe estate cars which could accommodate a wealth of kit, including folding signs, brooms, cones, lifting jacks, wheel braces, flashing lamps and searchlights the weight of which tested a vehicle's stopping distance. (*Metropolitan Police Museum*)

You're nicked! The police have foiled a wages raid with the driver of the Wolseley blocking in the gang's getaway Rover P4. Uniformed and plain clothes officers make sure that not all the bandits escape. The scene appears to have been contrived as part of a training exercise or as material for publicity purposes. Lifelike nevertheless, the illustration is evocative of the 1960s when Wolseley 6-99s and 110s were widely used by the Met and quality cars such as Rovers and Jaguars were often the choice of the criminal fraternity. (*Metropolitan Police Museum*)

This 1961 Morris Minor van is being used by West Riding of Yorkshire Police Dog Patrol. Note the ventilator on the roof. (*Colin Chipperfield Collection*)

This Standard Ensign estate car is in operation with City of Manchester Police, *c.* 1962. Note the twin bells. (*Colin Chipperfield Collection*)

MkIII Ford Zephyr 6s were introduced in 1962 and purchased by constabularies throughout the country. Ford made available special police models and could supply to particular specification. The car illustrated is in service with Essex Police who arrested the driver of a getaway van. (*Ford*)

Proving just how popular it was with police, Exeter Constabulary take delivery of the 1,000th 'police' model Ford Zephyr 6. The cars were comfortable and responsive and not surprisingly, drivers appreciated them. The cars were equally popular with mechanics. (*Ford*)

This interior shot of a Police Zephyr 6 shows the specially calibrated speedometer which was so positioned to be clearly read by the observer. The bench seat shows the car with a column gear change and near to the camera the radio equipment can be seen. (*Ford*)

In 1965 West Sussex used Ford Lotus Cortinas. At first glance there is little to tell these cars apart from production models – the familiar green flash along the body sides were missing – except for the tell-tale grilles, non-standard bumpers and wheels and, of course, the Lotus badges on the rear wings. For its day the Lotus Cortina had formidable performance with 103mph top speed. Ford supplied Cortina bodyshells to Lotus at Cheshunt where the engines, light alloy doors, bonnet and bootlid were fitted. (*Ford*)

Ford's rival Vauxhall also supplied special police models, this being the PB Velox. Powered by a 6-cylinder ohv engine, the top speed was 92mph; there was a choice of transmission: 3-speed manual with optional overdrive or 4-speed manual. (*Vauxhall Motors*)

The interior of the Vauxhall Velox Police model. Floor gear change was standard, along with bucket seats; the police calibrated speedometer was centrally mounted to be read by the non-driving observer and above it additional switches to control the car's auxiliary electrics. The radio is positioned in front of the observer's seat. (*Vauxhall Motors*)

Possibly the most famous 'policeman' in the sixties – Inspector Barlow of *Z-Cars*, alias actor Stratford Johns is seen here with a Mark IV Ford Zephyr 6, another police favourite. (*Ford*)

artbeat is another police drama series with a fond following. Although filmed in the 1990s and early 2000s it aptured' the 1960s. Contemporary cars were used, including this Rover 100. (*Author's collection*)

Training at Hendon encompassed all aspects of policing and police driving techniques. Police cadets who attended the Met's training establishment mostly revered their instructors; some aspired to become Class 1 drivers who were experienced enough to handle squad cars under even the most demanding conditions.

Hendon Driving School in April 1968. Pupils were put through their paces on the skid pan in a variety of cars including an early Mini, a Hillman Minx and a Wolseley 6-99/6-110. All the cars show evidence of battle scars (*Metropolitan Police Museum*)

This is the Wolseley police car as many remember it. The 6/80 was the backbone of many police fleets and despite its dedicated badging it had much in common with the M-series Morris Six. The car illustrated appears to have been used for publicity purposes as a number of official police photos exist using this vehicle. Pictured in front of a stately looking house, the driver and observer, who are unfortunately not identified, seem to be enjoying the occasion. (*Metropolitan Police Museum*)

Wolseley 6/80s were usually fitted with twin spotlamps, although in police guise the bell replaced the offside lamp. The engines on these cars were 6-cylinder overhead camshaft affairs, with an electric choke and a telescopic steering column among other features. Naturally, these cars had leather seats. Pictured on a wintry day in the mid-1950s, PGX 164 contrasts well with the surroundings. (*Metropolitan Police Museum*)

Even police cars suffer breakdowns and this Wolseley 6/80 is being transported to a police garage behind a Morris tow truck. Police garages were and are comprehensively equipped and manned by specially trained engineers and mechanics. (*Metropolitan Police Museum*)

In 1954 the Wolseley 6/90 superseded the 6/80. It had a twin-carb 2639cc 6-cylinder BMC C-series engine, torsion-bar front suspension with a coil-sprung live back axle. Wood and leather feature, of course, as does a four-speed column gear change. Series ll 6/90s were introduced in 1956 and Series llls in 1958; both models had revised rear suspension and a right-hand gear change on manual versions. TGK 314 is an Area Wireless Car and is passing the Cenotaph in Whitehall sometime in 1956; the taxicab is an Austin FX3. The Cenotaph was designed by Sir Edwin Lutyens RA and, according to a contemporary guide to London, 'every male passer-by will raise his hat'. (*Metropolitan Police Museum*)

was not unusual for the Metropolitan Police to enter the Monte Carlo Rally, a sporting event which summoned
 enthusiastic following and attracted well-known rally and racing drivers of the era. The 1956 team of officers
 m the Hendon Driving School, H.J. Shillabeer, G. Carruthers and E. Taylor, pose with their senior officer
 ngside the Met's 1954 Humber Super Snipe before leaving for Glasgow, their official Rally starting point.
 etropolitan Police Museum)

The Farina-styled Wolseley 6-99 was introduced in 1959 with a 102bhp 6-cylinder 2912cc engine; twin carbs, twin electric fuel pumps and servo front disc brakes were all part of the package. The Met used this and successor the 6-110, introduced in 1961, for a number of years. The 6-99 is illustrated here escorted by two so motorcycles.

Wolseley, one of Britain's oldest makes of motor car, was bought by William Morris in 1927, Austin a General Motors having also bid for the company when it faced bankruptcy. In 1935 Wolseley, together wi Morris, was absorbed into the newly formed Nuffield Organisation. Under the BMC regime, which broug together the names of Austin, Austin-Healey, MG, Morris, Riley, Vanden Plas and Wolseley in 1952, it was t last mentioned which often evoked so much nostalgia, although Riley enthusiasts would probably disagree.

The 6-99 was introduced in 1959 and shared much in common with the Austin A99; it was produced ur 1961 by which time in excess of 13,000 had been built. It had a Pressed-Steel chassis-body, independent fro suspension with coil springs, wishbones and anti-roll bar, as well as cam-and-peg steering and rear suspensi that comprised half-elliptic leaf springs. Typical performance was a top speed of 98mph and overall fu consumption of 19mpg. (*Metropolitan Police Museum*)

4

Motorway Patrol

If the early post-war years were noted for their austerity, then the second half of the 1950s and the 'Swinging Sixties' were remarkable for their prosperity. These were the boom years when British industry achieved much and the motor industry in particular prospered to the point that it was once world leader after America. Following the Second World War it had been a case of 'export or bust', when Britain's car manufacturers sold their products around the world in order to earn essential foreign revenue.

Britain's car industry certainly rallied to the cause and outwardly it had a phenomenally successful image. Behind the factory gates, however, the motor industry was in turmoil; it lacked any real sense of direction, nor was there sufficient investment for the future. The penalty was the gradual dissemination of the industry which, over decades, saw the disappearance of many respected and familiar names. The degree of innovation, design and technology that Britain's European competitors were demonstrating was largely being ignored at home; customers who often regarded foreign cars as being alien were happy, for the time being at any rate, to continue buying British.

The country as a whole built for the future, the reward being steadily rising standards of living. Huge acres of pasture and arable land gave way to concrete, bricks and mortar; cities spread, new towns were constructed, and there was a population boom. Harold Macmillan, then Prime Minister, told the British nation 'You've never had it so good' – he was right of course, despite no one actually believing him at the time.

As motor cars became not only more affordable, but more obtainable, despite quotas, import restrictions and purchase tax (double purchase tax on those models costing over £1,000), so the number of new vehicle registrations soared. Half a million new cars were sold in Britain in 1955 and within five years the figure nearly doubled.

The immense rise in vehicle numbers had, by the end of the 1950s, placed a significant strain on Britain's road system. Towns and cities up and down the country were being strangled by traffic vying for road space; it was not only cars that clogged narrow streets however, but delivery vans, lorries and buses. Vast amounts of freight were being transferred from rail to road, and while the former continued operating, for many businesses rail shipment proved costly and inconvenient. When Dr Richard Beeching, chairman of British Railways Board between 1963 and 1965, delivered his controversial report, the result was the near destruction of the rural rail network which accelerated the transfer of commodities to road transport.

In every part of the country those roads that led to the resorts were besieged by traffic on summer weekends and on bank holidays. Traffic queued for miles before it squeezed through bottlenecks and congested town centres. Arterial roads and by-passes directed through traffic away from urban areas and town centres, but autoroutes, similar to those on mainland Europe, were unknown.

The idea of a road linking London and Birmingham was first suggested in the 1920s, by motoring pioneer John Scott-Montagu, father of Lord Montagu of Beaulieu. Many people erroneously believe the M1, the first section of which was opened in 1959, to be Britain's first motorway. In fact the first section of motorway in Britain was the Preston bypass, now part of the M6, which was opened in 1958 to huge acclaim.

At this time Lancashire had the largest police force outside London. As a constabulary it had always been forward thinking, often establishing policies and evaluating equipment in advance of other forces, and having Britain's first stretch of motorway running through its boundaries summoned new and often controversial policing methods.

Spearheading the Lancashire force in the late 1950s was Col Eric St Johnston, a highly ambitious policeman who, before being appointed to Lancashire, was Chief Constable of Durham. During his term of office St Johnston had introduced radar speed traps to Lancashire's roads, an exercise aimed at reducing the numbers of accidents. Then St Johnston spent some time visiting several countries to view for himself different methods of policing. It was America that impressed him most and as soon as he returned to duty he was intent on introducing some of the policies he had seen.

The advent of a fast, expanding motorway network meant that it was possible to travel further and faster and to a degree in greater comfort than had previously been possible. Travel times were reduced and in comparison to today's traffic levels, motorways lacked relative congestion. The motorway age changed driving habits and while social motoring increased several fold, the rise in business related motoring was phenomenal. Consequently, cars were built to cover higher mileages at greater speeds, without necessarily incurring substantially more wear and tear.

In the early motorway days it was common to see pre-war cars abandoned on the hard shoulder and surrounded by clouds of steam and pools of oil. Vehicles ill-equipped for motorway driving were subjected to flat-out speeds in the outside lane (often referred to as the 'Jag-Lane') simply because the road was there.

The recipe of cars travelling faster on a wide new road without any speed restrictions could have spelled disaster, had it not been for a tough, but prudent, approach to road policing by Lancashire Constabulary. In keeping abreast with auto development, police, by necessity, frequently revised and updated their vehicle fleets and, with other motorways planned throughout the country, several constabularies took a keen interest in what Lancashire was doing.

St Johnston recognized that if his traffic police were to patrol a motorway efficiently they would need to be equipped with the latest vehicles. One thing that the Chief Constable had acknowledged from his visits abroad was that for motorway work police vehicles should be highly visible, so he had them painted white. The Home Office were slow to approve the change, which failed to deter St Johnston from his campaign. White police cars proved highly successful; the Home Office conceded and it was not long before other forces were following Lancashire's lead.

Just as white police cars had become an accepted feature on Britain's roads, Lancashire again set a precedent by conducting an experiment by painting them lurid orange – often referred to as 'dayglo'. As there were many more light coloured cars in the late 1950s and early 1960s, white vehicles no longer stood out. Again the Home Office disapproved, but Lancashire refused to be dissuaded and went as far as despatching one of its unmistakable cars around the country to gauge the opinions of constabularies and motorists alike. Despite the Home Office's initial reluctance to approve the colour scheme, several decades later the use of highly visible police vehicles has been fully accepted.

The vehicles employed by Lancashire for patrolling the M6 Preston bypass, together with the north and south extensions, when they were opened, included a fleet of MGAs. Replacing the TD and TF models, the MGAs were generally well received by patrol crews, despite some early fuel problems. At the time the constabulary was using low-octane commercial petrol, which meant that engines 'pinked' and ran-on after the ignition was switched off. To cure the problem drivers switched to premium octane petrol, which was obtained from selected garages, which transformed the performance. The first cars to arrive from MG's Abingdon factory were actually black, but were subsequently repainted white. Traffic patrol officers were supplied with white-topped caps from 1958 instead of the usual black variety; often nicknamed 'snowdrops', the caps were designed to provide Traffic patrols with a corporate uniform which blended with the new white and coloured vehicles.

The MGAs, while very capable performers, were not ideally designed for motorway patrols. Although they were highly manoeuvrable and commanded rapid acceleration, they were nevertheless limited in the amount of equipment they could carry. Once blankets, a two-way radio (which used a lot of electrical power and was responsible for many flat batteries), a couple of cones, warning signs and first-aid equipment were aboard, there was no space for the spare wheel. This was dispensed with and in the event of a puncture assistance from headquarters had to be summoned on the radio. The cars were not very spacious and patrol crews recall them as being cramped and uncomfortable.

Motorway patrol MGAs were mostly fitted with highly visible police signs; the front one was fitted with an amber, flashing emergency lamp and positioned immediately above the radiator grille ahead of the bonnet hatch. There was also another amber lamp on the front offside wing between the sidelamp and mirror. A rearward facing red lamp was level with the boot lid and incorporated a flashing 'stop' light. Looking almost out of place were two large public address loudspeakers, one positioned on the front offside bumper, the other on the offside rear. Other items of equipment included a tape measure, an incident box, a fire extinguisher, two white coats, two red hurricane lamps, four flares and two flare holders, as well as blankets and portable accident signs.

Drivers of white Lancashire Constabulary MGAs were expected to be in possession of an advanced (A) driving certificate, which was mandatory if they were to undertake motorway patrol work. Those drivers having the standard (B) certificate were confined to other traffic duties. Suffice it to say, the advanced driving tuition was conducted to very high standards, culminating in a rigorous test. Anyone who has taken the Institute of Advanced Motorists' test, which is usually conducted by a Class 1 Police Driver or Examiner, will be aware of the ability that is required. An ex-Lancashire Constabulary police officer and driving instructor, Jim Farmer, was employed by Rolls-Royce during the 1960s to foster safe driving at all levels within the company. Farmer's expert instruction was extended even to Rolls-Royce's test drivers who were recognized as highly skilled.

Lancashire pioneered the employment of women drivers, and policewomen were introduced to the sharp end of the traffic department at around the same time as the Preston bypass opened. Motorway duties were all part of their daily routine, as long as they were in possession of an advanced driving certificate. Those women police officers appointed to drive MGAs were frequently envied by their female colleagues in other forces.

Driving MGAs was not always as attractive as it seemed: in good weather during the summer it was enjoyable to have the hood lowered, but wet and wintry conditions were far from comfortable. On some days the cold was unbearable because the cars had no heaters, as radio sets had been installed in their place.

MG sports cars used for motorway work were eventually phased out, as they were deemed inappropriate. In reality, they afforded inadequate crew protection in the event of an accident, not to mention their unsuitability in poor weather. They were also ill-equipped to carry the ever-increasing amount of kit that was necessary and ultimately saloon and estate vehicles took over this demanding role. The redundant cars were transferred to other, but no less arduous, Traffic duties on trunk roads and for some time they remained a familiar sight on the busy A6, which stretched beyond Lancaster towards Kendal and the Lake District. MGAs were also widely used on the A45 Birmingham to Coventry bypass, which was once referred to as the most heavily policed stretch of road in Britain.

Experiments previously conducted around the country, using Humber estate cars to carry specialized equipment at speed to incidents or traffic accidents, promoted the use of such vehicle types for motorway patrols. Ford Zephyr MkII estate cars which, at that time were outstanding in design and carrying capacity, were introduced to Lancashire's vehicle fleet. These were ideal vehicles, for the cars' 6-cylinder 2½-litre engines provided around 85mph top speed, giving them the necessary power to transport the vast amount of equipment needed for motorway policing. Such items as tripod-mounted warning lights, a dozen marker cones, searchlights, collapsible accident signs, wide-load-ahead signs, crowbars, ropes, lifting jacks, tow ropes, blankets, torches, shovels, hand lamps, tape measures and measuring wheels were comfortably accommodated.

The Fords, like the MGAs, carried prominent police signs and public address speakers. The signs were fitted at either end of the roof, as well as blue flashing lights. Significantly, the cars wore large 'Police' decals on their bonnets, so there was no excuse for mistaking them for ordinary vehicles. The decals were also applied to the constabulary's MGAs to maintain a corporate identity.

The Zephyr estates must have impressed other constabularies, because when the M1 opened in November 1959, Bedfordshire chose seven Zephyr Farnham estate cars to patrol the motorway. The Met incorporated a number within its fleet, as did Cheshire for M6 patrols. The Zephyr and its sister cars, the Consul and Zodiac, were among the first British saloons to be fitted with power-assisted front wheel disc brakes. The option, costing under £30, was made available in time for the London Motor Show in 1960. Ford, like MG, were keen to adapt their cars to police specification, and made available a factory-built Zephyr police model with special modifications, including specially calibrated and accurate speedometers.

When the MkII Zephyr was replaced by the MkIII in October 1962, Ford again made available a dedicated 'police' model. These cars were never commercially marketed and were certainly not available to anybody except police authorities. Nevertheless, displayed on the Ford stand at the Earls Court Motor Show was a black Zephyr 6 in full police trim. Understandably, the car caused a lot of interest, not least among the many young boys and girls who dreamed one day of being a police driver.

Zephyr Police models had special exterior and interior fittings to include blue lamps and modified instrumentation. The specially calibrated speedometer was removed from its usual position, ahead of the driver, to the centre of the facia, in order that it could be easily read by the observer. Under the bonnet was the 109bhp Ford Zodiac engine and the rear axle had a 3.9:1 ratio, although the standard 3.545:1 unit remained available. The non-standard high speed nylon tyres, were fitted to heavy duty rims. A particularly interesting feature that was fitted was an alternator in place of the usual dynamo to accommodate the high level of electrical equipment aboard.

When Cheshire Constabulary ordered the MkIII Zephyr they specified the fitting of triple carburettors and Raymond Mays (of ERA and BRM fame) cylinder heads. Needless to say, Cheshire's Zephyrs were renowned for their impressive performance. The same constabulary also specified a few of its Zephyrs with a 'town differential'; it was recognized that some towns within the constabulary were somewhat hilly, and the low-ratio rear axle afforded far greater acceleration than would have been possible otherwise. While low-ratio axles did limit a car's top speed to no more than 70–75mph, the acceleration, nevertheless, was outstanding, especially when climbing hills.

All sources suggest that the Zephyrs were appreciated by both drivers and mechanics alike. The cars were popular with constabularies throughout the country and well over 1,000 special police vehicles were built.

Early in 1961 Ford took the first steps towards developing a new series of Zephyrs and Zodiacs, which emerged in April 1966 as the MkIV. The new models were available to police specification and Cheshire was one of the first constabularies to receive them. If earlier series of Zephyrs had been largely free of mechanical problems, alas this was not so with early MkIVs. The Cheshire force reported a catalogue of faults: in the electrics, wear of the front suspension struts, gear selector mechanism and braking system being the most numerous. It must be stressed that police cars usually cover much higher than average mileages, and that wear and tear on the suspension, braking and the gear changing mechanism was therefore commensurate. Ford quickly rectified faults and the cars lived on to provide lengthy and reliable service. Another matter which had given some concern was the handling in wet conditions attributed to poor road adhesion. The criticisms were investigated by Ford engineers who discovered the main problem lay with the tyres, which were made by Goodyear, the manufacturer having altered technical specifications at around the time MkIVs were introduced. Subsequently Ford specified a different Goodyear tyre for the model range as a whole and at the same time began to fit radial tyres to police models.

Police model MkIV Zephyrs retained the centrally located and specially calibrated speedometers from the MkIII. Whereas on the base model Zephyrs it was customary to fit a bench seat and a column gear selector, those specified for police use had bucket seats and a floor mounted gear change; between the front seats a centre console housed the radio equipment and auxiliary switches.

Lancashire police also used Land Rovers on motorways, which were particularly useful when towing broken down vehicles off the motorway, even pushing them when circumstance demanded and pulling wrecked vehicles out of the way of other traffic. Motorway patrolling was one of the first instances where Land Rovers were used for police work, though Rover cars had been used by constabularies over a number of years. Soon after their M6 debut similar Land Rover vehicles were purchased by other forces, including the Met.

Land Rovers were ideal as motorway police support vehicles and continue in use today. Used as fire tenders and field ambulances over many years, few had previously been seen in police guise. Liverpool City Police employed at least one Series II hardtop vehicle in 1960, the machine having been specially kitted out with roof-mounted ladders. Closely related to the Land Rover is the Range Rover which, since its introduction, has been extensively used on motorway patrols throughout the country. With their ample carrying capacity and formidable performance, they have for many years remained one of the most highly regarded of all police vehicles and are discussed further in another chapter.

Motorcycles were also a feature of motorway patrols because of their manoeuvrability and powerful acceleration. Unlike the car fleet, those motorcycles employed on the M6 were not initially in radio contact. Lancashire yet again were the driving force in this respect and in January 1959 were the first police force to introduce radio motorcycle patrols, following two years' intense development. Transistorized equipment enabled an officer to accept and transmit calls while on the move, which called for a specially designed helmet incorporating a headset which, in the event of the rider coming off his machine, would automatically disconnect.

To conclude the survey of early motorway policing, Lancashire were among those constabularies which opted for the 2.4 and 3.4-litre Jaguars. First announced in September 1955, in readiness for the 1956 model year, this was the first Jaguar to have unit construction. Its success was immediately assured, for it presented an essential sporting prowess, which was coupled with all the comfort of a family saloon. Good looking in town, the car, nevertheless, exuded that certain raciness which made it acceptable at the golf club. It was fast too: Jaguar's modified XK

6-cylinder twin overhead cam engine producing 112bhp, with the help of twin Solex carburettors, was enough to top the ton without over compromising fuel economy.

Within a few months the 3.4-litre was introduced. The performance potential of this car was amazing, for it had a top speed of 120mph, courtesy of the mighty 210bhp XK engine. The first cars were fitted with drum brakes, which had serious limitations when it came to some heavy-footed drivers, but any shortcomings were quickly overcome with the availability of all-round disc brakes. A sporting saloon par excellence, the 3.4-litre was the choice of racing drivers Mike Hawthorn and Duncan Hamilton, among others. Series ll models were introduced late in 1959 and a third variant, the 3.8-litre, was offered. For those motorists intent on speeding along new motorways, there was a shock in store, for the police too acknowledged Jaguar's potential.

As well as Lancashire, the Met had been quick to gauge the Jaguar's effectiveness. Examples were evaluated within the police driver training facilities and they also made an appearance with police departments throughout London. How many motorists can claim to have driven well in excess of the 70mph speed limit after its introduction on 1 January 1967, one eye on the road ahead and the other trained on the mirror for that unmistakable image of a white Jaguar . . . ?

Lancashire Constabulary were put under the spotlight when the Preston bypass was opened in 1958. This was the first motorway section in Britain, and the new road was a source of interest to everyone, including motorists and the police. The first link of the M6, the Preston bypass demanded a different approach to policing than other roads. The two cars pictured here could not be more different: MGAs were fast, but in reality were ill-equipped to cope with demands that motorways imposed, especially when it came to carrying specialist equipment. The Ford Zephyr estates were highly capable machines with a huge carrying capacity. Note that the cars are painted white, a policy pioneered by Lancashire Constabulary, which at first did not comply with Home Office directives. (*Greater Manchester Police Museum*)

The kit carried by Lancashire Motorway Patrol vehicles was comprehensive by 1958 standards, but limited compared with what today's police vehicle are expected to carry. No wonder that Zephyr estates (this is a MkII) were preferred to MG sports cars! (*Greater Manchester Police Museum*)

The M6 motorway, *c.* 1963. The carriageways are empty in comparison with today. Next to the MkIII Ford Zephyr is a solo motorcycle patrol officer, and in the air a BEA helicopter leased to the police for motorway duties. (*Greater Manchester Police Museum*)

A wide range of vehicles were put on motorway patrol duties in the early 1960s and an attempt was made to form a North-West Motorway Unit. In the foreground is a Staffordshire Constabulary Jaguar MkII saloon, certainly the fastest of the cars pictured, while the Lancashire MkIII Zephyr had little competition accommodation-wise. Police motorcyclists played an important role, as did the Cheshire Constabulary Land Rover, which had the benefit of four-wheel drive. The helicopter was useful in airlifting road accident casualties as well as directing operations to ground crews from the air. (*Greater Manchester Police Museum*)

For a number of years Greater Manchester Police used that stalwart the Wolseley 6-99 and its successor the 6-110. When the Range Rover was introduced in 1970 it became the ideal motorway policing vehicle and remains so today, being specified by constabularies throughout the country. The date of this photograph is unclear, but it is after 1981, as four door Range Rovers were not available until then. Note the GMP 999 number plates, as used by Greater Manchester Police for publicity purposes. (*Greater Manchester Police Museum*)

As the motorway network expanded constabularies used different types of vehicle for patrol work. This Austin 3-litre, not the most popular of cars, was used by the West Riding Force. (*Colin Chipperfield Collection*)

The type of kit carried by Greater Manchester Police in about 1981. Compare it with that carried by the Lancashire Constabulary in the early days of policing the M6 Preston bypass. (*Greater Manchester Police Museum*)

his Range Rover was operated by Greater Manchester Police, *c*. 1983. The beacon is certainly more effective an on earlier motorway patrol vehicles; however, compare it with the sophisticated units fitted to current types. *reater Manchester Police Museum*)

show of force by the Greater Manchester Police. When this picture was taken motorway patrolling had ogressed considerably from those formative years in the late 1950s. In addition to the Range Rovers can be seen Ford Sierra and a Vauxhall Senator along with a Sherpa Incident Unit vehicle. The familiar GMP 999 number ates can be seen. (*Greater Manchester Police Museum*)

The Range Rover was introduced in 1970 and has since become the benchmark for four-wheel drive dual-purpose vehicles. The vehicle's performance and comfort was convincing: it achieved 90mph and was smoother in operation than any other 4×4 then available. The Range Rover was entirely suitable for police use as it provided huge load capacity with sufficient power and speed to enable officers to respond to differing situations. Early models were heavy to handle, however, power steering, introduced after three years, made handling easier. Five door models were introduced in 1981 and two years later automatic transmission became available. A number of internal and external styling modifications, not all of which were welcomed by customers were introduced in 1984. A five-speed gearbox was introduced in 1983, and fuel injection for 1985/6; in April 1986 a turbo-diesel engine made the vehicle even more practical. After 1993 some significant changes were introduced: electronic air suspension and electronic traction control afforded a quality of ride and roadholding that make this one of the most advanced all-terrain vehicles in the world.

For many years Range Rovers have provided the means of patrolling motorways, this scene is pictured near Manchester around 1969. A number of police drivers preferred Land Rovers to Range Rovers because the former provided less roll when manoeuvring at speed. (*Greater Manchester Police Museum*)

5

From Cycles to Pandas

Changes to policing methods in the 1960s and 1970s largely brought an end to the bobby walking or cycling a beat. Just as the bicycle had immeasurably improved policing a century earlier, the motor car revolutionized community policing still further.

For years the image of the friendly bobby either on foot or on bicycle provoked many a caricature, both in the popular press and in the music hall: universally a plump individual with chubby cheeks and laughing eyes, not to mention a kind heart beneath a stern exterior, portrayed a safe perception. With the introduction of Unit Policing that symbol disappeared.

Unit Policing, or to be precise the Unit Beat System, was devised early in the 1960s more out of necessity than evolution of policing practice. The advent of new towns had brought about densely populated communities, often without any proper regard for localized policing. Whereas some new towns and large communities were without any police provision at all, some (in South Wales for example) had police offices, which had an altogether lower profile of administration than police stations, serving different housing estates. The two regions identified as having particular problems were Merseyside and Greater London. Kirkby, on the outskirts of Liverpool, has already been discussed in respect of mobile crime patrols, and despite new measures introduced to check the unwelcome rise in crime rates, an entirely different policing structure was necessary. It was often the case that there were simply too few town foot patrols and the only efficient way to police an area was to introduce mobile beats. In essence, five mobile beats were able to cover an area previously policed by eleven foot patrols.

In inner London estates of high-rise flats produced problems of their own, soon becoming notorious as dens of criminal activity and in a number of instances eventually being designated no-go areas.

The circumstances described here, while particular to certain localities, merely highlighted the constraints of urban policing generally. The slow plodding approach that foot and cycle patrols afforded were perceived as being outmoded in an era when the motor car was dominant. As the pace of life quickened the bobby on his bike was being left behind.

Alternative policing methods to make bobbies more mobile had been previously evaluated, and between 1962 and 1964 Stockport Borough Police introduced a novel but none the less effective idea. On a localized basis the police authority reverted to the once popular 'courtesy cops' theme within the community as an aid towards fostering good relations and to provide a more gentle approach to maintaining law and order. A small group of officers were appointed to the scheme and were provided with two-door Morris Minors, which were highly distinctive with 'Zebra' stripes across their bonnets.

Many people will remember the introduction of Velocette LE motorcycles ('noddy bikes') in the early 1960s, which were another way of affording bobbies greater mobility. The term noddy bike was not meant to be disparaging, but came about by default. It was customary for a constable to salute a senior officer, something which was not recommended while riding a motorcycle, so instead an officer was allowed to give a nod of the head.

The Velocettes were distinctive machines which were first introduced in 1948. Traditionally sturdy bikes, Velocettes competed with the best the industry could offer, so when the little-engine (LE) model arrived customers were confused. The company was convinced there was a strong demand for a minimally powerful, albeit tough and reliable, machine, embodying many innovative features to include a transverse water-cooled side-valve flat-twin engine. Possibly not designed for the committed motorcycle enthusiast, the LE was fitted with in-built dual level foot boards, ample sized leg shields, an angular pressed steel frame beam and a unique hand-operated starter (later changed to a kick-start) all of which, it was anticipated, would make it highly marketable. Initially having a 149cc engine, which was later increased to 192cc when comparative makes were 250cc, the LEs were seen as being somewhat feeble. The machines were fitted with three-speed gearboxes, which were superseded by four-speeds, but even that did not encourage orders. The LE did have its good points; it was mild mannered and the engine was so quiet that it hardly even whispered.

The LE's almost silent running, its reliability and easy maintenance were features which led police throughout the country to purchase several thousand bikes. In London and Birmingham, and indeed in many towns, noddy bikes were a welcome feature as they afforded real mobile policing without losing anonymity. Officers, in the main, appreciated them and felt less vulnerable than when riding a bicycle. LEs were in effect a forerunner to the Panda car. For police use Velocette were required to make a significant modification by fitting reinforced brake pedals to accommodate policemens' feet. However successful the Velocettes were, when Panda cars were introduced they became redundant.

Unit Policing in reality was not a new idea. William Palfrey (known as 'Palf') who was appointed Chief Constable of Accrington in 1947 had, just after the Second World War, foreseen that a requirement of policing would eventually entail a mixture of men on the beat as well as those equipped with high speed transport. Palfrey was able to put his philosophy to the test within Lancashire Constabulary under the command of the Chief Constable, Col Eric St Johnston.

Palfrey's doctrine proved highly successful and the crime rate fell dramatically during its trial period. Other divisions within Lancashire took note of the Kirkby experiment and were invited to adopt similar schemes. Simultaneously with the Kirkby project another scheme was being tested in Accrington. This was different inasmuch as foot patrols remained and beats were scheduled in accordance with local requirements. Beat officers were supported by teams of detectives who had responsibilities covering several beats.

In London a comparable scheme was under way with community officers forming an intrinsic part of an area police team. Living within districts they policed, officers were provided with personal radios in order that they could maintain constant contact with headquarters. Similar to their colleagues in Accrington, the London officers were backed up by teams of detectives.

The Kirkby project was the one that was most favoured by Lancashire's Chief Constable. Following intense planning, arrangements were made to introduce to the force a fleet of small cars suitable for Unit Policing. Obviously, there was no requirement for Traffic Patrol type vehicles, nor those used for Flying Squad duties. In essence, what was needed was an inexpensive and economical family-type car.

It was decided the car most appropriate was the 997cc Ford Anglia in its least expensive form and an order was given to Ford to supply 175 vehicles in time for the 1966 May Day parade at the Lancashire headquarters at Hutton. The cost of purchasing the cars amounted to £60,000 which, at a time when the car's basic catalogue price was £407, plus purchase tax, appears to have been good value. Several ideas had been discussed about what colour scheme to adopt: both black and white were deemed unacceptable because, it was decided, the vehicles should convey a positive identity. Oxford Blue was suggested – the Chief Constable had attended that University – but was considered too dark a shade, and ultimately either pale blue or turquoise were preferred. In making the cars even more identifiable it was suggested they had white doors with a corresponding white stripe across the roof, this emanating from an idea St Johnston had seen in Chicago where police cars were painted in contrasting colours.

When they were delivered the Anglias were known as Pandas, or Panda cars, an appellation which remains to this day. There are several stories as to how the name came about, but probably the most accurate is attributed to a journalist who, having spotted one of the distinctively painted Fords, likened it to a Panda.

The Kirkby experience had already produced some healthy publicity for Unit Beat Policing and the unveiling of the fleet of Anglias was too good a media opportunity to miss. When photographers and television crews arrived at Hutton they found the uniquely patterned Pandas positioned in '999' format. What gave the exercise all the more publicity was that the Anglias were built locally. Elsewhere in Lancashire, Wigan, in the interests of local policing, introduced a fleet of 1200cc Anglias, the cars costing £600 each. An officer was responsible for each vehicle, and was known as 'chief controller of their own beat'. In adjacent Cheshire, Ford Anglias were also specified; though most constabularies opted for blue and white colour schemes, in this instance green was chosen.

Mobility being the key to Unit Policing meant that the Pandas would be used to patrol areas both day and night and would, in some circumstances, be worked on a multi-shift system. Officers had the resourcefulness of the force behind them and that included the use of Lancon personal radios. This was yet another 'first' for Lancashire; personal radios were introduced in 1963 following trials lasting two years. As such devices were unavailable commercially at the time, Lancashire's own radio department had decided to develop the idea themselves. When it became a reality the concept was taken up across the country, revolutionizing foot patrols. The Met were quick to adopt a similar scheme, the radios then being known as Bat-Phones; in Birmingham Pye Pocketphones became standard issue.

Unit Policing was quickly adopted by other forces, so that by 1968 two-thirds of the British population was policed by this method. When Birmingham introduced Panda cars in 1967 the force had already carried out a successful pilot scheme in the city. Lancashire remained loyal to Halewood for orders of cars, so Birmingham remained supportive to Longbridge, purchasing a fleet of Austin A40 MkIIs. Birmingham's Pandas were painted a distinctive blue and white and were initially equipped with twin-tone air horns, as well as a blue beacon. The horns were a means of aiding movement in the city's congested streets, but were later removed. There were a number of reasons given for removing them, one being that they were passed to the fire service in the interests of economy. The real reason is that a number of Pandas were involved in accidents, and use of the horns had been a contributing factor.

The Anglias and A40s were two-door models which made them particularly ideal for police work. An absence of rear passenger doors and the ensuing security, was useful when conveying suspects and prisoners. In Countryman guise the A40 had the facility of an opening hatch at the rear, thus making it more akin to an estate car and the modern hatchback.

Depending upon local purchasing policies, the vehicles chosen for Panda fleets varied enormously. All were recognized British makes, and while a number of forces opted for Anglias some specified that model's successor, the MkI Escort; others preferred Vauxhall's Viva HA or the later HB series, with its larger engine capacity, uprated suspension, increased interior accommodation and more attractive styling. Then there was BMC, favoured by many forces who chose Britain's much loved Morris Minor 1000. Morris and Austin 1100s (the Austin was available a year after the Morris) were often selected because of their space-saving transverse engines and gearboxes built as a single unit, which drove the front wheels. The cars also featured Hydrolastic suspension which was unconventional. Front wheel drive, for some years a feature of many European cars, had, with the exception of a few notable examples, been largely ignored in Britain, and indeed many motorists remained sceptical and suspicious about such technology. The Issigonis-designed Mini along with the larger 1100s was instrumental in changing that perception.

Later generation Pandas included Escorts and Vivas; Morris Marinas were tried out by some forces while others opted to continue with the 1100s. Some evaluated the often criticized Austin Allegro, which initially sported the Quartic steering wheel, which was not round at all. Other vehicle types chosen included the Hillman Imp, with its rear-engine configuration and Rootes' answer to the Mini. Imps benefited from a nicely designed all-alloy engine and the gearbox was renowned for its smoothness of operation. Even so the car suffered from a multitude of minor

PANDA CARS: FORD ANGLIA AND MORRIS MINOR

COMPARATIVE SPECIFICATIONS

	Ford Anglia	Morris Minor
Engine:	4 cylinders, ohv, 997cc	4 cylinders, ohv, 1,098cc
Maximum power:	39bhp @ 5,000rpm	48bhp @ 5,100rpm
Transmission:	4 speeds;	4 speeds;
	14.8mph @ 1,000rpm, top gear	16.2mph @ 1,000rpm, top gear
Brakes:	Hydraulic, drum all round	Hydraulic, drum all round
Suspension:	F, independent, wishbones	F, independent, torsion bar and transverse wishbones
	Macpherson struts & coil springs R, live axle, s-e leaf springs	R, s-e leaf springs and live axle
Steering:	Burman Recirculating ball	Cam gears, rack and pinion
Dimensions:	OL, 12ft 9¾in	OL, 12ft 5¼in
	OW, 4ft 9in	OW 5ft 0in
	WB, 7ft 6in	WB 7ft 2in
Max. speed:	75mph	76mph
Fuel consumption:	39.9mpg touring	39.2mpg touring
	30mpg overall	36mpg overall
Fuel tank capacity:	7 gals	6½ gals

problems, including the pneumatically operated throttle, which adversely affected reliability.

There were some exceptions to the standard format of the Panda car. Not all vehicles were fitted with police beacons and did not have roof-mounted police signs. The configurations were varied and while most vehicles carried police decals on the doors, some Pandas were highly conspicuous, having both a police sign and a beacon fitted to the roof. Not all beacons were blue; some were amber, although standardization quickly came in. Blackpool was an exception to the rule, it retained its amber lamps for a longer period because they were more visible in the smogs for which the town was then renowned.

Unit Policing had its successes and failures. While crime rates fell initially, the trend did not necessarily continue. The fundamental reasons for introducing Unit Policing were often lost in the pressure to uphold the law generally and the role of the Panda car became more that of a police runabout than an intrinsic tool in area policing. Beat officers often became isolated from the very communities they were policing for the simple reason they were confined to their cars, and often their only contact with the outside world was by radio. The whole aspect of an officer getting to know a community and the community knowing their officer was lost. There was also a problem concerning confrontation with some people viewing the Panda car as an unwelcome figure of authority.

There were successes: Pandas provided the means of covering areas that otherwise might not have been policed and unit beat officers often dealt with 999 calls, leaving Traffic or Area crews to deal with other and sometimes more demanding incidents. However efficient Unit Policing proved to be, there was no substitute for foot patrols, in terms of direct contact. Throughout Britain the Unit Beat system was eventually abandoned and in some cases, sooner rather than later. As early as 1972 the South Wales force drastically reduced its car beats, of which there were 461. A revised policy put more area constables into the community and increased the number of officers walking the beat. That decision was later officially confirmed and the directive extended to other constabularies.

From Unit Policing there has been a move to Community Policing: modern technology, improved communications and the advent of highly technical police vehicles have revolutionized how much of the the country is policed. It was a good idea at the time, but the Panda car is no more.

Throughout the Unit Policing era many hundreds of Panda cars were supplied to police authorities. Vehicle manufacturers were naturally very keen to make available models designed for a specific purpose, usually basically trimmed and equipped to be sold at a specially low price. When forces disposed of their Panda fleets many vehicles were sold by auction to the used-car trade. Having always been treated to regular and thorough maintenance, these cars were a good proposition and a number of motorists enjoyed years of reliable use from them.

Before the Unit Beat System, which saw the arrival of the Panda car, police in Stockport operated a 'Courtesy Cops' scheme. The vehicles used were Morris Minors, painted in a unique livery suggesting a Zebra theme. The cars pictured here carry registrations issued in April 1962. The Stockport trials were carried out between 1962 and 1964. (*Greater Manchester Police Museum*)

e Unit Beat System was introduced in an attempt to provide more effective policing for urban areas and new vns and was initially centred on Merseyside. The system was deemed to be highly appropriate and was roduced to London and eventually to most urban areas of Britain. This picture illustrates a Ford Anglia Panda alongside a Jaguar S-type and Morris Commercial van of the Met. (*Metropolitan Police Museum*)

At around the same time that Unit Beat Policing was introduced, constabularies around the country purchased large numbers of Velocette LE motorcycles. The LE had many excellent qualities; nevertheless it failed to attract the number of customers that the manufacturer had anticipated. For police work Velocettes proved ideal; as well as being extremely quiet they were reliable and did much to mobilize the bobby on the beat. (*Greater Manchester Police Museum*)

This scene could be typical of many of the Met's fleets throughout the London area in the mid-1960s. On the left is a Hillman Minx, in the centre an Austin Mini van and on the right a Land Rover with a trailer on which there is a Velocette motorcycle. (*Metropolitan Police Museum*)

Ford Anglias built at Halewood were supplied to all constabularies, the first being dispatched to the Lancashire Force. This particular Anglia is pictured in Greater London, probably on the Kent borders. (*Ford*)

A fleet of Ford Anglia Pandas pictured at Chester. (*Colin Chipperfield Collection*)

Morris Minors, along with Ford Anglias and Escorts and other vehicle types were favoured as Panda cars, like these in Bristol. (*Colin Chipperfield Collection*)

The Met operated a large fleet of Pandas, all of which were painted a pale blue and white. The cars were specially provided by BMC and within the car the headlining unzipped to afford access to the roof-mounted police box. (*Metropolitan Police Museum*)

Hillman Imps were used by some constabularies, including Renfrewshire and Bute. Obviously there was some some local patronage, as the cars were built at Linwood. (*Colin Chipperfield Collection*)

The finishing touch. An Austin 1100 receiving final attention before being delivered to the Met. Austin and Morris 1100s shared much of the Mini's technology and were technically advanced in respect of their suspension and transverse engine and gearbox built as a single unit. (*Metropolitan Police Museum*)

Lincolnshire Constabulary were among those which adopted Unit Beat Policing. The idea was that an officer in a car had the resource to cover a much larger area than could otherwise be patrolled by foot. The problem was that officers usually became isolated from the sharp end of policing by virtue of being confined to a motor car. This is a MkI Ford Escort; the Escort family of cars survived until July 2000. (*Ford*)

West Riding Police used MkI Ford Escorts; these cars were fitted with beacons as well as police light boxes. Round headlamps were fitted on the De Luxe, which was the base model. Rubber mats replaced carpets and the facia was spartan with minimal instrumentation. (*Colin Chipperfield Collection*)

West Riding Police also purchased a fleet of Vauxhall Vivas. Note the poor fit of the door here. (*Colin Chipperfield Collection*)

When the Met disposed of its early fleets of Anglias and Escorts, the rather angular MkII Escorts, the car illustrated being the base model Popular, were purchased. Unit Beat Policing had its advantages, but ultimately the scheme was abandoned. (*Metropolitan Police Museum*)

Community policing has replaced Unit Beat Policing and the Panda car has given way to other vehicles using th
latest in automobile technology. such as the Ford Fiesta. Recent developments in communications systems mea
that police cars are in constant touch with constabulary headquarters. Stan Turbitt, a retired police officer, recal
the time when, in 1966, much patrolling was still done on foot assisted by pedal cycles and motor bikes and
number of cars and general purpose vehicles. Often it was only the older and more experienced officers who wer
allowed to drive. It wasn't unusual for a foot patrol officer to flag down a motorist, oust any passengers an
commandeer the car and driver in response to an emergency.

6

Blue Lights and Sirens

The familiar gong, a long tradition with police cars, but seriously outmoded in the 1960s, eventually gave way to a wholly more obtrusive warning, the two-tone siren. Ambulances and fire engines, not to mention coast guard and mountain rescue vehicles, were fitted with klaxons. Their introduction provoked some criticism from those people who were concerned about American influence in Britain.

It has to be said that an element of romanticism disappeared when sirens superseded bells, but they did so in the interests of safety. Imagine today being able to hear a gong in a busy city street when enveloped in our air-conditioned cars with the radio, tape or CD playing and surrounded by the cacophony of traffic.

By the time most police cars – Pandas excepted – were equipped with sirens, blue flashing lamps had become universal. Again this was a measure to make police vehicles all the more conspicuous, acting as a deterrent against speeding, crime and disorder. The transformation from bells to sirens was not immediate and for a period some vehicles employed both systems. There have been changes to the pattern and type of light boxes used on police vehicles; from the single blue beacon employed on Area cars, Traffic units normally had dual blue lamps and it was customary for these cars to be equipped with roof-mounted spotlights. More recently, and in the interest of safety, stem lights have been fitted which, as well as emitting a strobe effect, are more visible and incorporate red flashing lamps.

In the early 1960s such favourites as the Gerald Palmer-designed Wolseleys, Rileys and MGs gave way to the Farina-styled 6-99s, which were introduced in 1959 and superseded by the more powerful 6-110 in 1961. These cars were often used for motorway work in the early 1960s and were favoured by many constabularies. Crews liked them as they were extremely comfortable. Dependent upon budgets and buying policies of particular forces, the same family Austin A99s and A110 Westminsters were sometimes specified.

The 1960s were the heyday of the British Motor Corporation, and the giants from Dagenham and Luton demonstrated fierce rivalry. Rootes also had a long tradition of supplying Humbers to the police and Standard-Triumph which, in the opening years of the decade, were still supplying a few Vanguards and Ensigns to mainly provincial forces. Not all fleets comprised established British makes: the Met for example were using at least one Fiat 2300 and, all the more surprisingly, Citroën's highly innovative DS and ID19. The Citroëns were unique, and apart from their wonderfully charismatic styling employed hydraulic self-levelling suspension and a degree of roadholding which has since become legendary.

Several forces, including the City of Birmingham and the Met, used the Mini Cooper S which, as well as being very manoeuvrable, was exceptionally fast. Birmingham's Chief Constable was not convinced that the car was right for the job, however, and those within the fleet were disposed of after a relatively short service and a few miles, the last remaining example being decommissioned after 25,000 miles in May 1971. Cars then being evaluated by Birmingham for Traffic patrols included the BMC 1800 and the more powerful, but rather lumbering 2200, known within the force as the 'Giant Panda'.

The vestiges of British Leyland continued until the mid-1990s with the Maestro and Montego, badged as Austins and MGs, which were used by the Met and West Midlands. The hatchback Maestro seems to have been preferred to the Montego saloon and estate, if only because the handling and suspension afforded better performance and response. Metros were also Austin and MG badged, and some constabularies used the car in its basic forms for area and community beat policing.

Mention has been made of the Ford Zephyrs and Zodiacs and their adoption by forces throughout Britain continued with the MkIII and IV. The MkIV was something of a disappointment for Ford and when the company introduced its Consul/Granada replacement for the 1972 model year, several police forces incorporated these into their fleets. Base models, badged as Consuls, were fitted with 2-litre V4 engines, but it was the more powerful Granadas with their V6 2.5 and 3-litre engines that won police approval. Granada MkIIs were built from 1977 to 1985, the V6s having engines of 2.3 or 2.8-litres; the 2.8 fuel-injected version could easily manage 120mph. Cortinas were also used by some constabularies and in recent years the Sierra, Granada and Scorpio have all featured. The 4x4 and Cosworth RS Sierras were especially favoured, the latter having a maximum speed of 154mph. Escorts, Orions and Fiestas could be found in all areas of police work, mainly as modern day Pandas and area cars.

Vauxhalls also remained popular with police authorities, the Velox and Cresta PA series being characterized by their wrap-around front and rear windscreens and those distinctive fins, features that had some semblance with their American cousins. When, in 1962, the PA models were supplanted by the squarer looking PB, the series found its way into police fleets. Subsequent models such as the Cresta and Viscount PCs were purchased by some forces, as were the smaller FC and FD models; for motorway and rapid response use, it was the Carlton and Senator models which were most often seen. Cavaliers and Astras did much of the day-to-day community policing work, while, more recently, the MkII Carlton estates, with their massive carrying capacity, formed the backbone of many constabularies' motorway and trunk road patrols.

Rover featured among many fleets, and while the P4 75 and 90 models, which were acknowledged for their fine engineering, provided crews with exemplary comfort, they were hardly police material. When the 3-litre was introduced, itself a favourite with government departments, that too, along with the 3.5-litre V8, found approval in some areas. Rover really came into its own though in the mid-1960s with the introduction of the 2000 series, the 2000TC having more power than the original SC model. Handling and performance of these cars was exceptional at the time, and when the 3500 arrived in 1968, with its light alloy V8, it became the work-horse for many forces. Two years later the 3500S made its debut, with a top speed of 122mph. The model became synonymous with forces throughout the country.

When the Rover SDI was introduced in 1976 it was greeted with universal acclaim and it was only a matter of time before the police were using the cars in all aspects of rapid response and motorway work. The design of the car, with its hatchback rear, proved ideal; with the rear seats laid flat or removed altogether the cavernous interior easily accommodated the complex kit needed for policing. Even the early models were equipped with power steering and with V8 155bhp engines the top speed of these cars was in excess of 120mph. With specialist tuning they could achieve much more of course. Even the six-cylinder 2.3 and 2.6-litre engine cars were nippy and could reach 110mph, but it was the Vitesse that was really potent. With astonishing acceleration from 0–60mph in around 7 seconds, the car's top speed was at least 132mph. For years the SDI assumed the role of the archetypal police car.

When the SDI was superseded in July 1986 by the Rover 800 series, with its Honda connections, that too was adopted by police forces. Production of 800s was seriously behind schedule and therefore it was some time before police-specified models were delivered. Instead of having the familiar front-rear engine and transmission arrangement the new model had front wheel drive; Rover 800s and subsequent types have served the police well and many remained in service in 2000. V6 Rover 800s were capable cars and 130mph was well within their reach. The Vitesse with its 140mph potential was even more formidable than its SDI predecessor.

Triumph, taken over by Standard in 1944, was swallowed up in the British Leyland empire in 1968, by which time the 2000 saloon had been in production for some five years. From 1969 MkII models were adopted by a number of forces and in particular the 2.5Pl version was most popular. Triumph Vitesse saloons were also adopted, their sparkling performance being ideal for police work, and some were used as Q cars.

By the early 1970s Britain's motorway network had expanded considerably, and one of the busiest junctions, the Ray Hall Interchange, where the M5 linked the M6 in the West Midlands, opened. Shortly after, the Coleshill section of the M6 together with the Aston Expressway completed the Midlands link of motorways. Policing the 'Mid-Links' motorway system was shared by five constabularies and was conducted on a similar footing to that of the Regional Crime Squad. Two vehicle types, Range Rovers and 4.2-litre XJ6 Jaguars, were used to patrol the Mid-Links from a central base at Perry Barr. Both were highly capable vehicles, but it was the Range Rover, with its adaptability and colossal load carrying capacity, that was preferred. In other areas of police work the Land Rover, in its various derivatives, was popular, its load capacity and all-terrain capabilities being an advantage.

Elsewhere Jaguar was the hot favourite: most authorities had opted for the compact MkIIs, which were available with 2.4 or 3.4-litre engines and later the 3.8-litre. The 3.8-litre was so admired that Jaguar made vehicles especially to police specification. The trim level would have been unacceptable on production models; rubber mats replaced carpets, and hardboard panels substituted finely upholstered door panels. Many MkIIs were used for motorway duties and as it was necessary to carry such extensive kit, it was usual to remove the rear seats in order to increase stowage space.

When the 3.8-litre S-type was introduced in October 1963 police forces throughout the country took note. In essence, the new Jaguar was something of a hybrid, and while it shared certain styling similarities with the MkII it was nevertheless very different. S-types could be identified by their circular parking lights, elongated turn indicators and hooded headlamps. Heavier than MkII saloons, S-types were also slightly slower. Having a considerably larger boot and therefore greater carrying capacity, the car was attractive to some forces. The Met and East Sussex constabularies as well as Lancashire and Fife were among the first to adopt the model. While the vehicles were equipped according to force specification, most S-types were fitted with beacons as well as specially calibrated speedometers located so as to be easily read by the observer; other equipment included facia-mounted radio handsets and switchgear to control additional electrics, sirens and loud-hailers. The cars were invariably painted white, with decals in keeping with individual force requirements.

When the XJ6 arrived in the autumn of 1968 it presented the police with the perfect quick-response vehicle and one that was ideally suited to motorway patrolling. Series 2 cars, with the 4.2-litre engine were even more popular than the first models which had 2.8-litre engines and a relatively large number of the latter found their way into police fleets. The XJ6 enjoyed unmistakable styling; the car possessed a presence that was carried over to the interior appointments and police crews found the car relaxing to drive, even in arduous circumstances. The XJ6 had a 124mph top speed, although certain modifications improved this somewhat.

During the 1970s a number of constabularies evaluated some foreign makes of cars, in particular Volvo. Hampshire Constabulary operated a fleet of 144Es, which proved themselves on the county's trunk roads as well as the M3 motorway. Volvos continued to be used, especially the estate models which are acknowledged for their enormous load capacity, build quality and reliable engineering. Volvos are now very much part of the police scene with many forces specifying them. BMWs too had some following in some areas of the country.

Sports cars continued to feature and constabularies, especially Lancashire, the Met, West Midlands and West Sussex, incorporated MGBs into their fleets. Although some roadsters were used, it was generally the MGB GT that was preferred. When the MGC with its 3-litre engine made its appearance, it too found some favour, in both roadster and GT body styles, despite the model being short lived. The Met preferred the roadster version and operated some thirty cars while Lancashire opted for the GT, taking twenty-one into its fleet. When the MGB GT V8 was introduced in 1973, Thames Valley Constabulary purchased three cars and a further two demonstration cars were supplied to other forces for evaluation.

An unusual choice of car was the exclusive Daimler SP250 with its 2.5-litre V8 engine. This is the machine often referred to as the Dart, the appellation having been withdrawn by Daimler after Dodge, who had already used the name, objected to its use. The SP250 was acknowledged for its controversial styling, which had been created by Edward Turner. The sports car was also unusual as it had a glassfibre body and Daimler had hoped it would do for them what the XK120 had done for Jaguar. In the event that did not happen; the car was overshadowed by Jaguar's E-Type. In total fewer than 3,000 SP250s were built and a small number were adopted by the Metropolitan Police.

In about 1980 the Police Fleet Managers' Association was formed which, as a body, afforded greater specifying and purchasing arrangements. While the positive aspects of the association outweighed the negative, the prospect of using those vehicles which could be classed as excessive or exotic disappeared. In an age of accountability, the purse strings were tightly drawn. With the formation of the association the opportunity arose to largely standardize vehicle fleets, which promoted increasing use of multi-purpose vehicles. In recent years, therefore, the shape of the police vehicle has changed and more use has been made of vans, particularly Ford Transits and Sherpas. Area policing often relies upon small vans which are capable of dealing with almost any situation and therefore must carry a comprehensive kit.

During the last decade there has been much more reliance upon technology and all drivers in Britain will now be familiar with 'Gatso' cameras, so named after their inventor, the respected rally driver and Monte Carlo Rally winner Maurice Gatsonides. Advances in technology have made Gatso cameras obsolete, and a new system, known as 'Specs', has the power, via digital cameras, to calculate a car's average speed over given distances, and if that exceeds the limit the motorist can be prosecuted. This means, of course, that police have time to deal with other more essential duties.

The police have been responsible for detecting drivers under the influence of alcohol and it is more than three decades since the introduction of breathalyser tests. When stopping motorists police follow a code of conduct which is intended to maintain safety at all times. Many drivers have experienced that sinking feeling on hearing the wailing tones of a siren and seeing in the mirror blue flashing lights . . . and the relief when it is some other driver who is stopped!

MGBs were used by the Met and a number of other constabularies, including Lancashire, Leeds, Liverpool City, Devon, Glamorgan and the Royal Ulster. 106 FLY is seen here in service with the Met. It was used for publicity purposes on a number of occasions. (*Metropolitan Police Museum*)

Another view of 106 FLY, one of two MGBs purchased by the Met. Outside London some forces preferred MGB GTs. When the 3-litre MGC Roadster was introduced, the Met took thirty-one into its fleet; Lancashire Constabulary operated MGCs as well, but opted for the GT version. (*Metropolitan Police Museum*)

Along with MkII Jaguars, the S-types were a favourite with many constabularies. NVB 255E is pictured at speed while in service with the Met. (*Metropolitan Police Museum*)

Hooded headlamps and elongated turn indicators identify this as an S-type Jaguar. This model was often chosen in preference to the MkII because of its larger boot, the greater accommodation being appreciated when carrying the amount of kit required for Traffic patrol duties. Even so, it was often policy to remove the rear seats to make space for cones and signs. SUU 486F is seen here equipped with searchlights. (*Metropolitan Police Museum*)

Some of the Met's S-type Jaguars were fitted with E-type 3.8-litre engines and low-ration back axles to afford brilliant performance. Jaguar did not approve of the modifications, which were carried out by the Met's garage personnel, as they invalidated warranties.

This S-type Jaguar, WGK 475G, is on Westminster Bridge with Big Ben and the Houses of Parliament in the background producing an evocative image. These cars possessed not only good looks, but they were fine performers and could outpace most other cars of the time, especially with engine modifications which gave surprisingly athletic acceleration. (*Metropolitan Police Museum*)

Rover V8 3500s were popular with police and this example of a Met area car is painted Zircon Blue at a time when traffic cars were white. These cars shared similar styling with the Rover 2000 series, but were considerably faster. In the background is a Ford Anglia, of which many were used as Panda cars. (*Metropolitan Police Museum*)

Rover 3500 V8s (the model name being Three Thousand Five Hundred to dispel any confusion with the P5 3.5-litre) were derived by shoe-horning a light alloy V8 engine into the hull of a Rover 2000 to provide 117mph performance. Only the discreet badging and deep grille beneath the bumper suggested the car had more power than the 4-cylinder model, thus making this the ideal Q car, something which the police were quick to appreciate. (*Metropolitan Police Museum*)

Rover 2000 and 3500 models were often used by the Met on protection work and were allocated to select personnel, having responsibility for the safety of Royalty, visiting Heads of State and government ministers. Some other cars were also used for similar duties, including bullet-proof Rolls-Royce Silver Shadows.

Another version of the Rover 2000 the police used extensively was the TC (twin carbs), which provide 110mph performance. The crew of this car obviously enjoyed putting the vehicle through its paces. (*Metropolit Police Museum*)

When Jaguar introduced the XJ6 in September 1968 it was only a matter of time before police forces took the car into their fleets. West Yorkshire were operating this car when it was pictured in 1971 along an unfinished stretch of motorway. The fluorescent markings, which by this time were a feature of police cars, are shown to good effect. XJ6s were particularly liked by crews who appreciated the cars' comfort and performance. (*Colin Chipperfield Collection*)

Rivalling Rover, although by now under the same company umbrella, Triumph 2000s were specified by several constabularies. HJD 507K is a 2.5PI MkII saloon (the first series 2.5PIs were the UK's first fuel injected family cars) and is seen in Greater London when in service with the Met. With 138bhp engines these cars could easily exceed 100mph. (*Metropolitan Police Museum*)

Only subtle styling differences distinguish this Triumph Dolomite from the more basic 1500 models. West Yorkshire had a number of Dolomites in its fleet, promising good performance from their slant-four 1.85-litre ohc engines. Over 100 mph and sports saloon handling could be expected. (*Colin Chipperfield Collection*)

This Rover 3500 V8 is snapped at speed in the West Midlands. From an operating base at Perry Bar, W Midlands Police patrolled the 'Mid-Links', which was an area having parity with the Regional Crime Sqr Note the single blue beacon, searchlights and siren, as well as loudspeakers. (*Colin Chipperfield Collection*)

e 18-22 series of cars were designed to replace the BMC 1800 and 2200 models which had not achieved ticipated sales. The cars, it is said, lacked styling and performance. The car to succeed them was the ADO71; it as to be approximately the same size of vehicle, perhaps even larger. To have made it smaller would have nflicted with the Maxi hatchback. The styling engineer in charge of ADO71 was Harris Mann. He produced the :reme wedge shape which was well received when the car was introduced in 1975. The cars had front wheel .ve and Hydrogas suspension, they were very roomy and would have been highly practical if they had been signed with a rear-opening tailgate. The Princess version survived until 1981. This particular example is seen iile in operation with West Yorkshire Police. (*Colin Chipperfield Collection*)

Alan Keepax of 600 'A' Division Metropolitan Police is photographed with a new Rover 2600 SDI at Hyde Park Corner on 26 June 1978. The Met, along with other forces, employed the new shape Rover in quantity, as the cars served the police well. The SDI was the result of joint development between Rover and Triumph engineers in an effort to rationalize the BMC/BL range of cars to replace the P5, P6 and Triumph 2000/2500 models. (*Metropolitan Police Museum*)

By the time this picture was taken all Ford Granadas were being built in Germany. MkII Granadas were introduced in August 1977 for the 1978 model year and therefore the car depicted is an early example. The Granada range was complex, inasmuch as there were five model variations, a 4-cylinder 2-litre petrol, 2.1-litre diesel, 2.3-litre V6, 2.8-litre V6 and 2.8-litre V6 FI. The car illustrated is serving with Suffolk Constabulary. (*Ford*)

When the need arose it was customary for ambulances to have police escorts, in this instance a Rover SD1 of the Met's fleet. The Triumph-designed engines fitted to the 2300 and 2600 models were highly capable, the smaller, 123bhp unit, having a potential of more than 110mph. (*Metropolitan Police Museum*)

Having been introduced in 1976, the Rover SDI was voted Car of the Year in 1977. With its 3.5-litre engine made its debut in the wake of an oil crisis, this alone compromised initial sales. One of the car's most endearing features was its aerodynamic shape, it bore a striking resemblance to the front-wheel-drive Lancia Gamma. The SDI was styled by David Bache, one of Rover's most celebrated engineers, and the interior, again penned Bache, was distinctive with its box-like instrumentation on the fascia shelf. The car enjoyed brilliant performance and handling, which is one of the main reasons for it being adopted by police forces throughout Britain.

With blue lights flashing this Rover SDI 3500 is about to join a motorway in response to an emergency near Leeds. In the 1970s and 1980s these cars were a familiar part of the police scene, and no wonder for they afforded brilliant performance, with at least 125mph top speed and much faster according to tuning and specification. (*Colin Chipperfield Collection*)

ord Escorts, similar to this base model in service with Suffolk Constabulary, played an important role in beat
olicing. (*Ford*)

ice their introduction Ford Transits have served in most constabulary fleets. This is an all-wheel drive model
pable of tackling the most hostile terrain and is finished in special livery commensurate to Ford police
monstration vehicles. (*Ford*)

Sherpa vans rivalled Transits; this example is on duty on the approaches to the Westway, near Paddington i London. When this photograph was taken in 1985–6, increasing use was being made of multi-purpose vehicle (*Metropolitan Police Museum*)

Ford Fiestas found their way into most police forces to conduct mainly beat work. (*Ford*)

When Ford introduced a new range of Granadas in 1985 the company was quick to sell it to the police. Note the design on this 1987 demonstration model concept car. (*Ford*)

Ford Sierra Sapphire RS Cosworths made an ideal police response vehicle, especially with its 150mph top speed and acceleration of 0–60mph in 6.1 seconds. Here E522 CHK was in service with Suffolk Constabulary in 1987. Gone are the familiar beacons in favour of a stem affair. (*Ford*)

Ford Granada Scorpio 24Vs in a variety of police liveries, some with red side flashes, others with yellow and one, on the far right, with a blue and yellow arrangement. Chequered designs are also visible. This is a demonstration by Ford of some of the decals that could be specified. (*Ford*)

A Ford Sierra Sapphire Cosworth in Northumbria Police livery; the Tyne Bridge can be seen in the distance. (*Ford*)

Northumbria Police on exercise with an Escort RS Cosworth and a police helicopter hovering above a runway. Helicopters are used for a wide range of duties including road traffic accidents and pursuing criminals, including car thieves. (*Ford*)

Ford Mondeos were widely accepted as replacements for Sierras and Sapphires; this particular car is wearing Essex Police livery. The stem lights have a combination of blue, white and red lamps. (*Ford*)

A Ford Mondeo interior showing the auxiliary equipment and switchgear necessary for modern patrol work. (*Ford*)

Rovers continue a tradition of being specified for police use; this 800 series was operated by Devon and Cornwall Police. (*Colin Chipperfield Collection*)

Norfolk Police used Ford Mondeos for traffic duties. This officer is preparing to take a breathalyzer test from the motorist. (*Ford*)

While it has been practice to use a wide variety of vehicles, the police have traditionally used British vehicle where possible. However, times change, and as the global motor industry shrinks other makes and types are employed, such as this Volkswagen multi-purpose van. Note the interior cage, a feature of modern Black Maria VW Transporters have for a long time been used by police forces elsewhere in Europe, their reliability an surefootedness being much appreciated. The ubiquitous VW camper van, now built on a similar chassis to the vehicle illustrated, is one of the auto-industry's greatest success stories and is a familiar sight on British road (*Metropolitan Police Museum*)

e Bedford name originates from a decision by General Motors in 1931 to build a British version of its Chevrolet nge which was then being assembled at Hendon. It was at Luton, home of the Vauxhall works, that production Bedford commercials was established, and during the Second World War the factory helped produce some 50,000 Bedford trucks for the war effort. New models announced in 1953 departed from a decidedly pre-war age, not only was styling all new, but serious modifications were made to running gear, with Perkins diesel gines an option to petrol types on vehicles of over 4 tons capacity. In 1954 General Motors opened a new truck int at nearby Dunstable and 1957 saw the arrival of a series of trucks and tractor units known as the Big dfords. Forward-control trucks were introduced in 1960, prototype vehicles carrying the GMC name having en seen in mainland Europe for some time.

Austin Gypsy vehicles were recognized for their utilitarian qualities and were favoured by the utility companies, e authorities and the police. However, they never acquired the same charisma or recognition as Land Rovers. anchester and Salford Police employed a varied fleet of support vehicles, including this Bedford Incident Control it. Behind is an Austin Gypsy with a compressor trailer. (*Greater Manchester Police Museum*)

This scene is typical of the early 1980s, showing a variety of vehicles in use with the Met. From left to right can be seen a Sherpa van, an Austin Metro, an unmarked Vauxhall Cavalier, a Mini van and a Rover SD (*Metropolitan Police Museum*)

This photograph typifies the fleet operated by Greater Manchester Police in the mid-1980s. In the back row is a Sherpa van, two Land Rovers and a Ford Transit; in the front row is a Ford Sierra estate car, a Sierra saloon Peugeot, a Range Rover, another Sierra and a Bedford van. (*Greater Manchester Police Museum*)

7

Police Vehicles Today

The modern police car is a complex and highly technical vehicle, having to adapt to many demanding roles. All constabulary fleets comprise a range of vehicles which are selected for particular tasks, and therefore a car intended for mainly beat work would be ill-equipped for patrolling motorways or for rapid response situations which might end in high speed pursuits.

With the need for police authorities to be highly accountable, the debate over finance and public spending is forever in the spotlight. There is a move towards using multi-purpose vehicles wherever possible which can be used as area cars, people carriers, general purpose carry-alls or, when the need arises, as armed response units. The social and geographical nature of a constabulary will have significance on those vehicles purchased: a force having a largely urban territory, such as London, West Midlands or Greater Manchester, will have quite different operating requirements to, say, Cumbria, Devon and Cornwall, Northumbria, Wales, Scotland and Ulster. Those constabularies responsible for policing extensive networks of motorway will have their own particular needs, which do not always exist in other parts of the country.

Beat vehicles are likely to be small to medium sized saloons or hatchbacks, while substantially more powerful machines will be found undertaking rapid response and motorway duties. Vehicles in the latter category would normally be at the leading edge of technology, having decisive acceleration together with impressive top speeds, usually in excess of 130mph. The criteria of course is to be able to match the performance of other vehicles; thus police fleets are continually being revised and updated.

Cars such as Vauxhall Corsas and Astras, Ford Fiestas and Focuses, together with the Peugeot 306 and Rover 25 and 45 will often comprise beat fleets, although others will be employed. Such vehicles might not always have on-board communications, but the officer in charge will have a personal radio.

Where multi-purpose vehicles are specified, the choice is rich and varied. Traditionally, Ford has led the market with the Transit, which is available in many derivatives from a humble general purpose van or mini bus to a specially designed

4×4 all-terrain unit capable of various roles. Ford Transits have long been used as the modern Black Maria, now more often referred to as 'Saturday Night Specials', and are factory-built and fitted out with 'prison cells'. At the moment Mercedes and Peugeot are gaining a market share. There is increasing use of new generation MPVs, including the Vauxhall Frontera and the smaller Zafira, both of which undertake motorway patrol work as well as other equally demanding policing. Ford's Galaxy and Explorer are popular with some constabularies, the manufacturer supplying to order special versions including those fitted with gun boxes for armed response work.

Land Rovers and Range Rovers, long associated with the police, remain an essential ingredient in many forces. While the Land Rover, be it Freelander, Defender or Discovery, can be adapted for various duties, it is the Range Rover which is mostly specified for motorway duties. Other vehicles, including those not usually associated with the police, are constantly being evaluated and include Jeep and Honda. West Yorkshire Police at one time was using a Russian Lada Niva 4×4 for service in the Holmfirth area.

Rapid response cars are evaluated for their performance in accordance with each force's needs. While high powered medium-size saloons might be ideal in conurbations, others, such as Range Rovers, Ford or Vauxhall 4×4s and large Volvo estate cars, might be better used in more rural areas.

Most constabularies operate a wide range of quick response vehicles, the more popular being the Ford Mondeo ST200 and ST24, Vauxhall Vectra V6, Omega and Volvos. The Ford Mondeo ST200 has outstanding acceleration (0–60mph in 7.5 seconds) and 135mph performance – courtesy of a 2.5-litre (2495cc) 202bhp V6 engine. Not all forces require such massive power and may choose the marginally less athletic 168bhp, 2544cc ST24 with its maximum of 131mph. Vauxhall's Omega also has a choice of V6 engines, 2.5 and 3.0-litres, and according to specification can reach in excess of 150mph. Volvo, now incorporated under the Ford umbrella, is being more widely specified than it once was. The V70 estate car and its predecessors have long been used for motorway and trunk road patrols, their power, performance and commodious capacity making them ideal for this purpose.

Rovers continue to be used and although the 800 series has been supplanted by the new 75, these vehicles still have a life ahead of them. It is customary for constabularies to evaluate widely different machines as they become available, including Saab, Subaru, Nissan, Peugeot, Toyota and Volkswagen.

Support vehicles form an important part of any fleet and these can include Dog Unit vans, such as the Ford Courier, which are suitably equipped for transporting animals. Additionally, incident unit vehicles which have to cover a huge range of duties all have to be accommodated within constabulary administration.

All police drivers undergo a special programme of training which, at the end of 2000, was standardized throughout the country. There are two levels of instruction, standard and advanced, both being intensive and based around two manuals, *Roadcraft*, and *Human Aspects of Police Driving*. In both cases the tuition ensures candidates adopt the correct attitude, as without this failure is certain.

The right attitude is one of a calm, considered and professional approach to driving under all conditions and tolerance and consideration to other road users –

and that includes recognizing one's own limitations and abilities. Driving to a system is important, as are observation, planning and awareness. Use of controls may seem academic, but when this is coupled with high speed driving, often under stressful conditions, proper use of gears, brakes and steering is essential, as is the necessary use of signals. Tuition is not just about handling a vehicle under normal conditions: skidding, motorway driving and an in-depth knowledge of procedures are critical.

Drivers of quick response vehicles are highly experienced and in addition to having undergone extensive training are in possession of a Class 1 Police Drivers Certificate. The crews of such vehicles have a detailed knowledge of the area in which they work; they also have first-aid experience and can usually deal calmly with any situation which might be encountered, and that includes the use of firearms, which are kept safely on board.

Today's police cars are equipped with powerful communications systems. Because of changes in the way the police service is administered, some regions have fewer police stations than there once were, which means that police vehicles, by necessity, are self-contained units which are in permanent contact with control centres. Technological advances mean that satellite tracking can identify the whereabouts of a particular vehicle, thus aiding security as well as managing response systems.

Vehicle technology means that reliability is ensured, and because of longer service intervals cars are off the road considerably less than they were years ago. Advances in fuel economy without compromising performance helps to check running costs, and this adds to overall efficiency.

Modern police vehicles are expected to undertake hugely diverse workloads. Depending upon location, of course, this can vary from accompanying large loads, escorting heads of state, airport and seaport security, conveying prisoners and so on.

Constabulary vehicle workshops are finely equipped to conduct all types of servicing. Some have facilities for accident repairs, although some forces use external specialists for such work. Sometimes vehicles arrive from manufacturers ready to enter service, while others, according to their role, undergo modifications. Electronic and special communications systems are mostly installed at constabulary workshops, and it is amazing how much additional equipment a car is expected to carry.

When it is time for police vehicles to be decommissioned they are stripped of their constabulary decals and all police equipment is removed. Mostly the vehicles are sold at auction, usually to specialist agents and there is often a keen market for them. Sometimes purchased by police vehicle enthusiasts, they can form the basis of an excellent acquisition. While the mileage of such cars is normally high in comparison to their age, they will have been expertly cared for.

Northumbria Police conducting speed checks on the outskirts of Newcastle upon Tyne from their Ford R
Sapphire Cosworth. Scenes such as this were commonplace until the arrival of Gatso cameras, which in the ear
2000s are currently being superseded by an altogether more sophisticated digital system of speed detection. (For

One of the more unusual types of police vehicle is this Lada Niva 4-wheel drive, pictured on 1 April 1999 near Holmfirth, West Yorkshire, where *Last of the Summer Wine* is filmed. This vehicle was purchased for the local bobby by the community, as the surrounding countryside is hilly with terrain that is difficult to negotiate. (*John Black*)

This model Granada Scorpio, in service with Hampshire Constabulary, was short lived. Since the mid-1990s it has been withdrawn from the Ford catalogue, hence few were sold to the police. (*Ford*)

Seen at Stansted Airport, this Ford Galaxy armed response vehicle was photographed for publicity and demonstration purposes. Nevertheless, police are only too aware of the need to be vigilant at airports and airfields around the country. Note the vehicle's four headlamp system and the front facing blue auxiliary lamps, combined with the side mirrors. (*Ford*)

The useful amount of space in the rear of the Ford Galaxy is evident; multi-purpose vehicles such as this are becoming increasingly popular with police. (*Ford*)

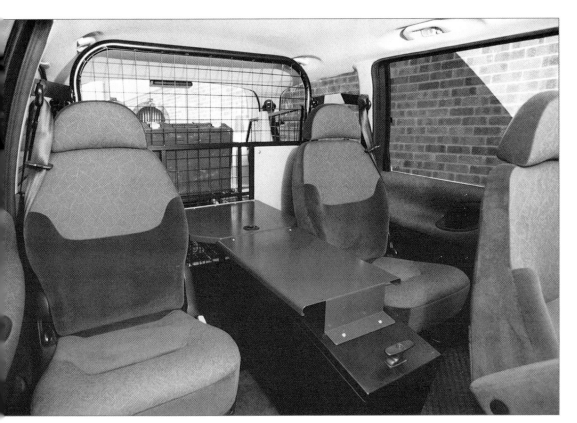

e interior of a Galaxy armed response vehicle, showing the gunbox positioned between the rear seats; behind
e division can be seen some of the equipment carried for Traffic duties. (*Ford*)

ıxhall introduced the new Astra police beat cars at a special launch event at Donington Park. These models
specially available to constabularies and cannot be otherwise specified. (*Vauxhall Motors*)

Police constabularies evaluate vehicle types in response to particular needs. Cars such as the type illustrated off prove ideal in areas of fairly high population density; a compact carry-all being what is required to present effective police presence. The Zafira is one of a new generation of small multi-purpose vehicles, this example is police motorway livery. (*Vauxhall Motors*)

e Vauxhall Omega is popular with the police and is available in various engine configurations. The most
werful models provide effortless performance, making them ideal for motorway and rapid response work.
uxhall)

Fiesta-based Ford Courier can be specified for many uses, including a purpose-built Dog Unit vehicle. A police
handler is pictured while evaluating this Ford demonstrator. The dog seems happy! (*Ford*)

'Saturday Night Specials' is the name given to these Ford Transits, which are in effect modern Black Marias. Ma specifically for police work, the vehicles are built and fitted out by the maker. (*Ford*)

Kent Constabulary took delivery of a fleet of new Ford Focus hatchbacks, four of which can be seen outside county's police headquarters. (*Ford*)

...ex Police were among the first constabularies to opt for the new Focus estate car which offers maximum ...ommodation, a necessity when patrolling motorways. (*Ford*)

...o of Lothian & Borders Ford Focus saloons pictured alongside an Escort MkII Panda car, which is painted in ...familiar blue and white colour scheme. (*Ford*)

Ford supply the police with a number of high performance Mondeos, this being the ST24 with its 131mph t
speed, used by Kent County Constabulary. (*Ford*)

Even more powerful than the ST24 is the Mondeo ST200. This is a police demonstrator fitted with a 2.5-litre
engine capable of 135mph and accelerating from 0–60mph in 7.5 seconds. (*Ford*)

nbria boasts one of the toughest and most isolated terrains in England, so the police employ a variety of icles to match these testing conditions. As well as Volvo estate cars, the police fleet includes Vauxhall nteras, Ford Mavericks and Explorers, as well as Land Rovers, Range Rovers, Jeeps and Subarus. *thor/Cumbria Constabulary*)

Peugeot Partner is just one of several multi-purpose vehicles belonging to Cumbria Constabulary. Peugeots, in icular the 306, are extensively used for beat work. (*Author/Cumbria Constabulary*)

Volvo cars made their appearance in 1927 and since then have been recognized for their engineering quality.
first post-war car was the PV444 and was also the first to sell well outside Scandinavia. It was that car more th
any other that acquired a reputation for good roadholding and construction quality for the company. New mo
followed and in 1967 the 144 was introduced with a range of safety features previously unseen on most c
Volvo cars today are synonymous with reliability and longevity.

Here is part of Surrey Police's fleet of Volvo estate cars. These vehicles, while renowned for their excell
performance, reliability and build quality, form an essential part of the constabulary's motorway patrol unit
the M3, M23 and M25 run through the county. (*Volvo Car UK*)

A Volvo V70 police car publicity and demonstration vehicle. Volvos have been used in the UK for many years. Saloons at one time were used to patrol the Hampshire section of the M3, as well as other roads in the county. The V70's impressive load capacity and spirited performance make this one of the most popular police vehicles. (*Volvo Car UK*)

Tail piece. A familiar sight on roads and motorways throughout Britain: this modern police car is with Hampshire Constabulary. (*Volvo Car UK*)

INDEX